Mastering Short-Term Rentals: The First 50 Tips You Need - Vol. 1

By Nick Kirov

Dedications:

Not really sure how to start here. I will keep it nice and short for everyone. You will read a bit about myself and what I have been through in my business journey and a bit about my life in the next chapter, but in this one I want to take the chance to express my gratitude and appreciation to the people because of whom I am the person I am today and I have the opportunity to be doing what I do. Both my parents – Tania and Dilyan – have been there to support me throughout my childhood, adultery and the "mature years" of my life. They have been the team that has supported me in my business journey from day 1.

Even though we have had many arguments and struggles throughout the years – it has been their support that allowed me to build something for them, work on growing it and get closer and closer to allowing them to leave their dream life. We are halfway there. Not long until one of my Dream Goals becomes a reality...

Also I want to mention that I have upmost respect and love for the people in my closed circle – the people I consider part of my familia – Isso, Sakata, Nick, Ra, Julia, Alex, Nana, Atanas, Piotr, Ventsi, Drago, Nicole. Knowing that you know and have people that you can rely on is a rare thing to have in this world. I am happy I have that!

To the ones I have not mentioned here and we are close – probably you owe me one more coffee before you get into the close circle – so I'll be waiting for the invite!

And finally but not on the final place – I would like to thank myself! I would like to thank the 21 year old me that has made the decision to get this life together, step on the path to personal development and fully focus all of his energy into building something that will last for years and years to come! And that is not the business – that is the person I have become today. And you know what? This is not the end! Only the beginning!

About the Author:

At the time of writing, the author – Nick Kirov – is 25 years old. He was born and raised in Bulgaria, but moulded and made in the UK. He came to the Southampton, UK when he was 16 years old. Only thinking that he was here on a vacation for the summer holidays, he later realised that he ain't going back. Started college and he hated it. For the 1st year he wanted to go back every single day. But that day never came. After he saw that he had no other choice but to give UK a try he delved into educating himself and following some sort of a career that he was not even sure what that might have been. Making the final decision between IT and Sport – he chose to go to a college where he would play basketball and become a professional basketball player. Spoiler alert – that never happened...

When he went into college he was doing sport and fitness. Being into health and fitness himself, he decided that he can abandon the "possibility" of a "professional" basketballer and get himself in becoming a Personal Trainer. Another spoiler alert – he did... but not for long.

After graduating college with 3x Distinction * he signed up for university all across the UK – to some of the most prestigious universities that teach Sport Science – Exeter, Loughborough, Chichester etc. Very excited about it – he went to a few of the opening days where the professors were meant to "sell you" on their University and the subjects you were going to study. That unfortunately did not happen.

After working at his job behind a desk in an Amazon warehouse (part time hours – remember – someone at that age could not only study – they had to work as well!) – he was bored one day and as a typical Bulgarian person would do – he opened Google and typed in the phrase that would change his life – "HOW TO MAKE MORE MONEY?"

And just like that the all-knowing website gave him the answer that he needed – or the answers shall I say – many answers – answers such as:

-assets

-liabilities

-gold and silver

-stocks and bonds

-real estate investing

Guess what he did then?

He went to Google again and started researching each and every word that Google gave him previously – what is assets, what is liabilities, how to invest in stocks and bonds, is real estate investing possible for a 19 year olds?

After so many answers came out from just that one search – a book appeared in front of him that changed the courses of his professional and academic career that he was planning on taking – the book was called "Rich Dad, Poor Dad" by Robert Kiyosaki.

After reading that book – he had to make a choice that could most likely disappoint his parents and make them think – what will you be doing with your life if you don't go to university? And you guessed right – he called all universities that he applied for (and got accepted in all of them) and declined their offer for acceptance. He chose that he would prefer to spend money on self-education and pay someone that is doing the exact thing that he wants to do, rather than spend 3-4 years in university and not knowing what he will end up being in the end + learn from professors that know everything by the book and most likely never had a professional career in sport. Did he made the right decision or not – only time will tell.

After reading that book , Nick got interested in educating himself on money and investing, self-development, positive mind set and believing in something that is so far to reach that he could have called it day dreaming. Regardless to what the case was – Nick was motivated to make those 3-4 years that he did not go to university and turn them into something positive for him and his family.

After finishing college – he went from part time to full time working – in another manufacturing company. However, working 12 hour shifts for 4x days on and 4x days off were not enough for him, so he tried working as a Personal Trainer in the gym on his 4x days off from the main job. As well as learning and educating himself on money mindset.

Fast forward 6 months – Nick was already getting familiar with the PMA mentality (Positive Mental Attitude) and educating himself on property investing that a good friend of his invited him to attend this property investing seminar in London.

Excited, he booked days off from both work places, and attended the 2x day event and off the back of it he was so excited to have learned the different strategies about property investing that after he came back he started researching how to buy a property up north (Nick was living in Southampton), because properties are much cheaper to buy. The only problem that he realised was stopping him from doing that was – you needed a deposit to get a BTL (Buy-to-Let) property. A deposit Nick did not have.

Scratch that – buying a property up north was immediately off the table. Nick needed another option – another low cost entry into the property investing game that would be able to get him his first "passive" income – and that option was R2R (Rent-to-Rent).

After doing all of his due diligence on Rent-to-Rent, learning through all the books, online videos and posts he could find, he thought he was ready to jump on a call and speak with an agent to secure his 1st R2R deal.

1st call went like this:

Agent: Hello XYZ Agency speaking, how can we help?

Nick: Arrhhg Hello, erm, I am Nick and I, uhm want a property to rent and rent it to other people... please?

You can only imagine the demotivation that Nick felt after the agent laughed on the other side of the line and hung up.

Devastated, Nick went into reading more and watching more videos on property, without even realising how much he was procrastinating. He should have made the 2nd and 3rd and 4th call until he reached the point of being more comfortable on speaking on the phone and actually get those viewings scheduled with these agents for him to go out of his comfort zone, speak with those agents and secure a deal… but that is not what happened.

Only another 6 months later needed to get by, until Nick finally got his 1st Rent-to-Rent deal. And this one was a R2SA (Rent-to-Serviced-Accommodation). He was so excited about it that he did not realise that after the agent agreeing to the terms and rent, Nick was meant to pay for getting the keys (rent + deposit) and staging the property (furniture + decoration) to which he had no money to spend. Fun stuff isn't it.

Before understanding how powerful networking can be, Nick was trying to find ways to gather the cash for getting his 1st deal done and dusted. So he did what he thought was his only option – he went to the bank and got a loan out (just want to say – what I did, I do not recommend anyone else of doing, it is what my only option at that time was). 15mins later, £4k landed in his bank account. Poof. Just like that and Nick had his first cash to pay the agent for the contracts and legals, source furniture, redecorate the whole flat, and still have some cash left for when the property was done if there were no bookings within the 1st month.

Excited and scared at the same time – he went out and finished his 1st R2SA property and called it Poseidon Apartment – The Heart of Town

It was a beautiful and small 1x bed / 1x bath apartment in the city centre of Southampton – in the exact same building where Nick lived the 1st year he came to the UK – a coincidence – not really sure about that!

Within 10 days of finishing with the 1st project, the 1st reservation came through for 2x nights – 3x months from now. Then another one came in a few hours later for 14x nights check-in from after a few days from now. Nick was finally reaping the rewards of all of his hard work. But was he really now?

2x days before the 14x night booking that he got, Nick came back from work and he received another reservation – for 1x night – for this night – check-in after 1 hour (keep in mind it was about 7pm already). Oh, forgot to mention – 4x guests wanted to stay in the 1x bed apartment. Was that a red flag? Maybe, but was it a foolish mistake of letting that group stay and them wrecking the place on the next morning when you went to check all of your hard work go to the bin? Who might have known right?

A mistake that could have easily been avoided if a 2x night minimum was a standard procedure + a damage deposit taken – but who does that on their very 1st Airbnb apartment?

And so, after the long night has passed and the next morning Nick and his cleaner went to check how was the property- they found out that there was a party going on that night that Nick as the host did not even get invited – what a shame…

Balloons and confetti everywhere, drinks spilled on the carpet and kitchen worktop, toilet paper thrown everywhere, dirty dishes, food and juice spilled over the bed – seemed like they have had plenty of fun that night. Best thing is that someone needed to clean all of this and get the property ready for the next guest that was checking-in only a few hours later and would have stayed for 14x nights.

Property got sorted quickly, freshly prepared for the new guest and lesson was partially taken from Nick. Partially, because the same situation needed to happen again, before he realised that there needs to be some security measures in place.

After this big booking was done, there was smaller bookings coming in – this is a dream come true is what Nick was thinking. "PASSIVE INCOME" is a real thing!!! Not until a mysterious "deadly" virus struck and shut the whole world down in the end of March 2020. Yes, COVID-19 was the reason why the Serviced Accommodation Industry and the Travel and Tourism sector suffered massively. Travel Agencies were blocking their calendars, planes stopped flying, no tourists were coming to town, only "key workers" were eligible to work. CHAOS!!!

However, if it wasn't for this CHAOS, and getting through one of the most toughest markets for the Serviced Accommodation/Short Term Rental industry, that Nick realised that there ain't no such thing as "passive income". Nick had to actively work into trying to keep his property filled with guests. He even joined a small mentorship programme to teach him how to pass through those tough times. It was tough...

More on what exactly happened during the Corona years and how Nick managed to stay afloat and endure those difficult times – reach out to him on all socials – Nick Kirov.

Coming into 3.5+ years of Nick running his Serviced Accommodation / Short Term Rental business – he has accumulated over a dozen properties spread across Southampton and Portsmouth. Doing R2SA, R2R HMO, Assisted Sales, SA management, running his own Cleaning Business, working with 2x business partners, managing a small team of 3x people and getting the biggest growth within the last year of him running his business and bypassing the £ ¼ million turnover mark – Nick is happy to share his top 50 tips for the beginner/intermediate/advanced Serviced Accommodation / Short Term Rental guy/gal!

Introduction to SA

What is SA, Serviced Accommodation, Short Term Rental, Furnish Holiday Let, Self-catering accommodation – pretty much the same thing. You will hear me say SA throughout the rest of this book. What I am referring to is – SA is an alternative to a hotel, where people can book a room, apartment, house, villa, cabin or whatever else you can think of and stay there during their holiday, work, relocation whilst buying or selling a house, transit between their next flight, cruise etc. Without complicating stuff and confusing you – SA is a property where people stay, pay you money, then when they leave you need to clean and prepare it for the next guests. As simple as that. But as I said – it is simple, but not easy to do. Or are least, it isn't easy until you start!

Currently, there are over 30 million properties that are being offered only on Airbnb and Booking.com alone! That is crazy! And if you can control a few of your own – do you think that can get you outside of your day job? Sure did for me!

Adapting the Rent to Rent strategy I mentioned earlier to the Short Term Holiday Let market is something that is very affordable and realistic even in the 2023 post Pandemic marketplace. I started my business before the world went quiet in 2020 and passed through one of the toughest times for running a serviced accommodation business. Today there are huge opportunities to get into this space with little to no money and take advantage of this booming opportunity within the property industry.

It's like if the property industry and the hotel industry had a baby – that'll be the R2SA strategy (Rent to Serviced Accommodation).

So what exactly you need to do after you have secured your first property?

Once you have the keys, you need to make sure that the property is up to a modern standard all throughout – bathrooms, kitchen, and bedrooms. You need to make sure that all the walls are painted using fresh colours – and no, Magnolia is not a fresh colour!

Then after its all refreshed, you need to furnish it – this is where your creativity can flourish – you can use your imagination (without going too crazy). Or you know what – f*ck it – paint the ceiling pink, get your yellow pillows with your blue carpets and red table fitted – your property will definitely stand out – for good or for bad. But honestly, the furnishing and decoration of the property is the second best thing of doing Serviced Accommodation. You want to know what is the number one best thing? Keep reading!

After you have decided what the theme for your property will be and you have furnished and decorated it, now you need to have your professional photos taken and update your listings over the travel agencies out there – Airbnb, Booking.com, Vrbo, Expedia, Trivago etc.

Uploading your first property online can be a task that can be boring and annoying. But you only need to do that once or twice – I can show you later on how you can systemise this process, so you don't have to do it for each one of your new properties.

After everything is up and running – now it comes the fun part – GETTING BOOKINGS and GETTING PAID! Afterall, why have all of this hassle of trying to negotiate the deal, work on your numbers, paint the property, buy the furniture, set it up nicely, pay for professional photos, add everything to the travel platforms and not get paid? No point right?

That is exactly why when you do get your first booking, and that cash lands in your bank account – all of your efforts were worth it! And do you want to know what the cherry on the top is? When your guest checks out and they write to you and leave you an amazing review of how they loved your place, your attention to detail, the way you made them feel with your outstanding customer service, understanding their needs and desires and all of that sums up for an overall awesome experience to them. Do you think they will book and stay with you again in the future? Oh yeah! Without a doubt! Just make sure you keep their data. Oops, I'll tell you about this in a bit.

A very important aspect of the this business model I forgot to mention earlier and it is probably appropriate of saying it now – after you already have had money coming in to your bank account – is the setting up of your running costs aka "the bills". Yes, this is the notorious word that unfortunately for many of you, keeping me included, is and has to be mentioned within this book. I will not be giving you a step by step of how to set them up and which companies you need to go for, but I will tell you this: the bills will form a big part of your "fixed monthly expenses" when running your SA business. The main things that you will be paying for when you get your first property is – rent, gas and/or electric, water, internet, council tax/business rates, insurances. The secondary, and maybe for you – not so mandatory expenses when starting out are: TV licence (optional), security systems (optional), channel manager (optional), dynamic pricing systems (optional), payment merchants (optional).

When you are starting out – I would recommend you do your numbers only on the primary fixed monthly expenses. If you already have got a few properties under your belt – have a look at adding the secondary ones as well.

And here you go – now you have your 1st property ready – you've got guests paying and staying with you, you have your monthly expenses set up and you are ready to check my top 50 SA Tips below! Hope you find some of them useful!

50x Tips On Mastering Your Short Term Rental Business

Tip #1 – Start With Your Exit

What does that mean? To start with the Exit is something that everyone needs to do when they go into any business endeavour – to keep it simple – when you get your R2R property – most typically you would like an agreement of 3 to 5 years. Having this will ensure that you keep control of that property for long enough so that you can recoup your initial investment back and start profiting from it for a longer time. However, what if the property does not work, what if it is in the wrong location or this business just is not for you? Now you are locked in a 3 -5 year agreement that you cannot break out?

Wrong! This is where the magical term "Break Clause" comes in! To have a Break Clause in your agreement between the landlord/agent means that at whatever point you say – 6 months, 12 months, 1 month of the signing of the agreement, you (and/or your landlord) can break the agreement and exit the contract without any fees or fines being paid.

So let's give you an example. You sign this 1x bed flat in Manchester with the agent for 3 years term with a 6 month break clause. So you setup the property within the first few weeks, start getting bookings, and by month 4 all the bookings have disappeared. Nobody is booking, you are getting negative reviews for your property... All hell breaks loose. Or does it? What you have to do now is tell your agent that you would like to activate the Break Clause on your contract on month 6. This then allows them to start looking for a new tenant and allows you to either sell or move all of your furniture out of the property. Month 6 comes in, you get the keys back to the agent – no hard feelings. And you move on.

This is why knowing that you have a plan B if things don't work out is a good option. Obviously do not go with the mindset that it is not going to work, because what you project is what you get.

Tip #2 – Who Is Responsible?

You need to know who is responsible for what when you get your first property to run as an SA. When you sign directly with the landlord it is only you and them – so communication should be fairly easy. When there is an agent in between you – communication slows down and sometimes it can be misinterpreted when it gets delivered to your landlord. So, how to fix this?

In your contract that you sign it needs to state clearly – whose responsibility is for what around that property. Who needs to pay if there is a small leak under the kitchen tap or if the boiler breaks? This will be stated in your contract, but you need to put yourself in the position – if some maintenance problem occurs – who pays for what and how much. For example – in most of our agreements we cover small/minor maintenance problems up to £100. So if there is a leak somewhere, or an electrical problem with a socket, or the toilet needs unblocking – that is mainly on us – we do not even bother asking the landlord to check it, because by the time they come over, we might already have new guests waiting to come over the property, but your toilet is blocked so you cannot let them in.

No such thing – we source it out immediately after that happens with our power team of trades professionals. They come over – identify the problem, sort it out, they send us an invoice, we pay it and it's done and dusted. However, if you have a bigger problem – let's say the shower cabin glass breaks and you need a complete new shower panel that will cost a few hundred pounds, or the boiler breaks and they might need to repair it and/or buy a new one which will cost them a few thousand pounds – it is their responsibility to do.

At this stage when that major problem occurs you experience the beauties of running a hotel like business – your guests do not have hot water and no heating and it is -20 degrees outside – what do you do when your landlord is on holiday in sunny Thailand? If you are to follow your contract – your landlord needs to sort this issue, right? Wrong! You are responsible for what is happening within the property, because at the end of the day it is your business that is going to suffer. So what do you do?

You have a few options – you either relocate your guests at your other properties (if you have any), or you find someone else that does the exact same business as you do and relocate your guests to them. At the end of the day you will have to take the hit, but your guests will remember what you have done for them and will still leave you a good review.

You can always carry on doing the works yourself and still invoicing your agent/landlord for all of the works done. But keep in mind that the likelihood of them paying you the invoice in time, and not messing up with your monthly cashflow - it's kind of impossible. But it is an option that you can use.

Tip #3 – Be Quick With Resolving Maintenance Problems

So, you've received a call from your guest at 10am this morning telling you that the heating does not work. You tell them to check the boiler and they tell you that it does not seem to be working. What do you do? You tell them that you will get your plumber to come over and have a look right? Correct.

After you speak with your "trusted plumber" – he tells you that he has a few jobs in booked until about 4pm today – then he will come over and have a look. You seem to be happy with that and tell your guests. So far so good right? Okay, 4pm comes around and your plumber tells you that he is running late – has to pick up the kids from school and then he is on his way. You put yourself in his shoes and completely understand him. 5pm is around the corner. You call him again and he tells you that he is in massive traffic and will probably be there about 6pm. A bit frustrated, but still understanding, you tell them okay – you will wait for them. The guests at this point have not had heating nor hot water all day by the way. Anyways – 6:45pm you get a call from the plumber saying that he just had a flat tyre on his car, his cat is on her period, his wife just gave birth in the hospital and there is an offer on the new FIFA 23 for half price in his local supermarket only today. So guess what that means – he ain't making it to your property today. And that heating problem you had – yes, you guessed that right – it ain't being fixed today. And do you remember about that guest that you promised that the problem will be fixed later today – yes, they are all frustrated, already looking at another alternative accommodation, asking you for a full refund and cannot wait to give you a negative review.

So, what do you do? Is it the plumber's fault that they cannot make it today? Is it the guests' fault that the boiler does not work? Or maybe his cat got her period at the worst time of the month? No – neither one of them. It is your fault for not seeing this through. You should be prepared to find 101 solutions to 100 problems that can happen on a daily basis within your business.

So let me tell you how to avoid this from happening. When I get any type of maintenance situation – let's say we stick with the boiler problem – I do this. I call Bob the plumber – he tells me he can come over at 4pm. I book him in. Then I hang up and call Jo the plumber – he tells me can possibly make it for 3pm. I book him in. And then what do I do? Yes you are right – I call John the plumber – and John tells me that actually he is in the area and can come over within the next 30mins. I book him in as well. So, what happens now?

When John comes in at 10:30am and checks the problem – there are 2x possible outcomes. The least likely one of them is that John would not be able to fix the issue. Are you happy now, that you know that Jo is coming over at 3pm and has a better chance of fixing the problem? And if he can't, then Bob will be joining in at 4pm. So you will get 3x opinions of what the problems is and what can be done about it. However, the most likely scenario that you will encounter is this – John will identify the problem – tell me what it is, how much it will cost and when can he get it fixed. If the answers to those questions are – minor fault, not gonna cost a lot and I can do it within the next hour or 2, just gonna need to pop to the shop and buy the parts – then yes – do it! Get them to fix the problem. Then you call Bob and Jo and tell them that you need to cancel that appointment.

Next time – when another maintenance occurs – call them 3x people again (if the job requires a plumber of course) and book them in, starting from either one first. Let's say Jo fixes the problem this time. So you just made business with John and Jo. 2x positive transactions took place. This means that every time you call them up – again and again and again – they would like to do more business with you.

And let's get back to the fun part – a lot of you might think – this is so immoral. How can you call someone, book an appointment and then cancel it? They would never want to do business with you ever again! That is perfectly fine by me! I need to look after my business first, before makings sure all plumbers out there feel good because of me. Take control of every maintenance situation by acting quick – having a power team around you – be fair to your tradespeople and understand that your guest is the number 1 person that you need to ensure has a great experience whilst staying in your property.

Tip #4 – Know Your Area

Have you heard the expression – LOCATION, LOCATION, LOCATION? Yes, this is a very real concept in a lot of businesses out there. Knowing your area and choosing the right location for your property is key! But how do you do that. Everyone will tell you – do your "due diligence" in the area, and then you will know if it will be right or wrong.

There are multiple ways to do that – I will give you 2x examples.

1st what you can do is – open up Booking.com or Airbnb – check which areas are most likely to have more property – the saturated the area- the better – there is a reason why everyone wants a short term rental on that street – because IT WORKS. You have to be careful though with choosing an area that has a lot of properties – but neither one gets booked. Yes, you see this all of the time – the photos of the property have been taken with a Nokia C3 camera at a 75 degree angle with a flashlight – ewww. Wonder why they ain't getting any bookings? Or probably the area is one which has higher crime levels? But how do you check that – have a look at this website below to know any street's ins and outs on demographics, crime levels, etc:

https://www.streetcheck.co.uk/

The 2nd way of checking if an area is good or not is to see if there are any local hotels nearby – guess what. You know your lil market research that you have done – are people looking to stay in my city, what sort of demographic I will be getting, how much can I charge them? Guess what – that hotel on that street – they have spent MONEY on finding that out FOR YOU! And you just got that information from them! For FREE! And if you want to dig even deeper into this – you can call the hotel – and tell them you need 10-20-30 rooms next week for a 7 days and possibly for the next few months. You are a business and have employees that are relocating in the area to work. You can ask them their AVAILABILITY, their monthly average OCCUPANCY, their NIGHTLY RATE. Basically, all the information that you need to know if anyone of the nearby properties will work for you based on those figures. You are welcome!

Also, a lil bonus to this – when checking which area in your city to choose from – know this. Your guest has a very low chance of knowing which areas are good and which areas they need to avoid once they come to your city. If you were to have a scale from 1 (very bad area) to 10 (safest and prettiest area) – your properties can be in and about the 5-7 on that scale – as long as you don't get shot or stabbed once you get outside of the accommodation – your guest will surely appreciate that! And a final bonus tip – promise it will be last – areas that work best are – close to any hospitals, construction sites, big arenas or stadiums, city centres, close to airports and train station. Anywhere that you have good access to transport links and there is a lot of work (construction sites) or foot traffic (city centres, malls) is always a good bet.

Tip #5 – Give More Than You Offer

What does this even mean? To give more than you offer means exactly that. When you take a property from your agent/landlord – you promise that you will look after the property, sort the small maintenance issues and pay them rent every month without a fail. So they know it will be a no brainer if they decide to go with someone else that will wreck the place after 12x months when they normal tenancy expires. And probably miss a few rental payments to them.

If you take a slightly distressed property and you tell the agent/landlord that you will bring it up to good standard, because you need a good, clean and modern looking property for your business to run smoothly, they don't care that much – they just want the safe money. However, after you have done up the property nicely, put some fresh paint on, furnished and decorated it beautifully, and go and show them photos of what you have done – now they see what you meant by "bringing it up to a good standard".

Now they see what you are all about and can entrust you with more properties. But do you know what is even better? 2x years later during your agreement with them, you ask them to come over and have a look at the property again – and it is still kept to an amazing quality and standard or even improved from the last 2x years the photos were taken! This is when they realise they have made the right decision to choose you as their "tenant"!

After you have that trust built and that proof of concept that you are serious at what you do – then they can start giving you more properties or speaking with other people they know that can offset you more properties. And just from that 1x agent/landlord you can build quite a good portfolio of R2R properties that you manage as Serviced Accommodation!

Tip #6 – Build Trust

How do you build trust with your lettings agent/landlord? Is it as simple as telling them – "you can trust me!". If it was that easy – everyone out there will be a salesperson. In order to build trust with someone – first they need to know you, then they need to like you and finally can they get to trust you. So how do you progress through this 3x step process?

Through consistency and perseverance. First, those agent need to know who you are – this can be done by you calling them up regularly, booking viewings and seeing the same agent over and over again. With time you can build rapport with them. Without transferring this to a sales book, you also need to know how to interact with them – get them to speak more and you listen (everyone likes to talk about themselves, so if you can make them talk more – they will like you more – simple as that), laugh with them, cry with them (when needed), but make sure you are being genuine in your interactions – everyone will spot a fake laugh and see when you are trying to be manipulative.

So to recap – get them to know you once you've spoken over the phone multiple times, view a few properties, build rapport and next time a property comes across to them, you might be the lucky one that receives a call from them asking you if you want to view it!

Wait, what about landlords? Some landlords don't have multiple properties and are advertising only 1x house/flat. How can I get them to trust me when I will probably see them only once?

That is where you are wrong. You will not see them only once, and you will not speak with them only once. Consider the landlords as "cold leads". Not being a sales book, but take notes – cold lead is someone that might not be interested at what you are selling, because they might need more information from you, more credibility, more proof that you are not a scammer. And they are in their full right to think this way – come on, at the end of the day who opens up a company yesterday and tries and pitch to a landlord that you will "guarantee" the rent, make sure it is "professionally" cleaned, deal with "all" minor maintenance issues – it is just too good to be true.

This is exactly why you need to turn that "cold lead" into a "warm lead". What do I mean by this? Well, simple – put them at the "back burner" whilst you carry on looking for other properties with other agents/landlords. And check-up on them – every few months. See how they are doing, is their property already rented – you are still around if they might be interested in giving you their property and renting it out to you.

If you already have had your first deal – you can always send them a few before and after photos of this property that you just completed on last month and tell that this is something that you can do for them and their property. This will build your proof of concept and because you have been "warming up" that lead – they might be the ones that will give you your next deal... or next 10x deals. Who knows?

Tip #7 – The Deal Before You're Compliant

So many people look into getting their "ducks in a row" as my mentor used to say and they are not focusing on the main thing that will bring them money – getting the DEAL. "But what about if someone decides to sue me or I get fined or they ask me but I don't have my documents ready yet?".

Let's be honest – nobody will prosecute you if you pick up the phone and call an agent to book a viewing for you. Nor they will fine you when you tell them that you opened your business yesterday. With every new endeavour you undertake you will always lack confidence at the beginning – the main reason for that is that you do not have the knowledge or experience yet. So yes, you will feel uncomfortable and scared. But try to avoid that from stopping you from picking up the phone or attending a few viewings – yes, the first ones will be sh*t. How do you think my ones went? The agents asked me questions that I was not ready to answer, one landlord told me that he used to work this other company that went bust and he had a bad experience with giving his properties to a company especially at their early stages. What do you think I said to him? Nothing – 10x seconds of silence. 10x long seconds of silence. It was a very awkward moment. I was just not ready nor knew what an appropriate answer will be. I have been there. But you know what helped me?

Knowing that after each 'No" I get, I am closer and closer to the "Yes" I need. And linking this back to being compliant. Your main priority is to get the deal and get the money. After having the money, then you get sort your insurances and guarantees and systems and all of that. Focus on finding your next deal. Confidence will come through perseverance.

Tip #8 – Refine Your Agents

You want to know which agent's understand your business model and are happy to work with you, but you don't want to deal with constant rejection? This is what you can do. It is a 1 hour long exercise, but once it is done, you will most likely not have to do it again. Go and grab a pen and a paper. Write down in 3x columns – Yes/ No/ Maybe. Then go on Google and write down your city – let's say Bournemouth letting's agents. Then you press Enter. Voila.

Now you have all 20-30-40 agencies in your city that are connected to landlords in your area and are offering properties to rent. So far so good. Now what you need to do – probably the scariest part for some of you – is to call each number on that list of agencies. And wait till you reach someone. After you speak with an agent and you pitch them – depending on their answer is where you are going to add them to that list you made earlier. For example – you tell them what you do and if they start asking a lot of questions – probably they are on the fence, but not sure yet – add them to the "Maybe" section. If they say they are okay with what you are planning to do with the property, then they are your "Yes" agencies – those are the people you want to speak with and get to build relationships with. If they say "No" however, you will put them under the "No" section, but you can target those properties in another way – I will explain in another tip later.

And that is it! 1 hour later and you filtered through all of those letting's agents just like that. Now, all of this data that you have you will use when you call those agents again.

Tip #9 – Pass The Gatekeeper

Who is the Gatekeeper? Is that the old man Gandalf from Lord of the Rings you need to be dealing with? How did his name come into this book? Let's get back to the point – the gatekeeper is the agent (most of the time – the newest and inexperienced person) that is sat at the very first line in the office and taking most calls when people call the office. Take a note of the word inexperienced. Do you want to pitch the inexperienced person, which is most likely to say "NO we are not able to help you", because he does not understand what the hell you trying to say to him. Of course not!

What you need to do is bypass him/her and get into the professionals that do the viewings and are actual letting's agents. So, how can you do this? When you jump on a call and Jim picks up and asks how he can help. You tell him – Hi Jim, can you pass me onto the lettings team please? This is it. As simple as that. But, wait, it couldn't be that easy though, could it? Of course it can – the property game is simple, you don't have to overcomplicate it! "But what if they start asking you questions before they transfer your across" is what you may ask? Well you answer some of them and don't answer others. Let me give you a few examples:

Me: Hi Jim, can you pass me onto the lettings team please?

Agent: Hi there, no worries, is there something that I can help with?

Me: Yes Jim, if you can pass me to someone at lettings that will be great!

What if the people from the lettings team are all out on viewings or busy on the other line? Well, you tell Jim that you will call later and you hang up. You DO NOT want to be talking to Jim about how you are going to get a property from them and then rent it out and then guarantee the rent and look after the maintenance and clean it professionally. No! Jim does not know what you are talking about.

Don't get me wrong – you don't have to be a d*ck to Jim, just try and bypass him, because you don't want to be wasting your time explaining yourself to Jim, whilst you can be calling another agent and already booking a viewing for tomorrow. Sometimes if you have already spoken with someone from the lettings team – say her name is Sally – you already have a name there. So next time you call and Jim answers the phone – ask him if you can speak with Sally. He might then probably think that you and Sally have spoken and know to pass you to her as a matter of urgency (you might have already viewed a property with Sally and might be interested in taking it, so he would not want Sally to lose on her commission of getting a property to you, so Jim will make sure Sally is available to speak with you.

This is how powerful getting a name from the correct people is. It opens a lot of doors and bypasses the Gatekeeper much easier.

Tip #10 – Script It & Pitch It

Do you remember back in school when the teacher gave you for homework to write a word 100 times in order to remember how to write it, or learn a paragraph that you needed to recite in front of your classmates? Have you ever wondered why that was? Do you remember the kid that never sat down to learn that

4 sentence text and he sounded awful with the uhms, and erms? How unprofessional and undisciplined that sounded? That is how you sound on your first few phone calls to the agents/landlords.

See it this way – they are professionals – they are dealing with many landlords and tenants and investors on a daily basis, Monday to Friday and sometimes even Saturdays – saying the same thing over and over and over again. Do you think it took them years and years to learn those scripts? Hell no! A week probably? Just to get the gist of what they are saying?

Yeah, exactly! They had a script that they read of from when they started, then they adapted it to their personality and character and now it comes out naturally when they speak. So why don't you do the same? Write your script down. Practice it in front of the mirror. Over and over and over again. Call 5x of our friends and pitch it to them. Get them to give you an honest opinion whether or not you sound like a robot or it sounds all natural and relaxed.

Remember what Bruce Lee said one - "I am not afraid of the man who knows 10,000 kicks but only done them once, I am afraid of the man who practiced 1x kick 10,000 times". You need to practice the same pitch over and over again until it becomes natural to you. And no, you do not have to practice and remember the whole A-Z conversation – you need to be confident in your introduction and pitch. Then you will see how the conversation will go. You will have different objections every time, but you can write down the most common ones and practice of overcoming them one by one.

But just remember – knowing your pitch, having a script that you go from, learning it and adapting it to your own style of speaking – this will present you in a better light and put you in a better position to get a viewing booked when speaking to the lettings agent/ landlord.

Tip #11 – Book a viewing immediately

It is your 157th call this week and you have your very first lettings agent that is happy to book an appointment for a viewing of that property that they can let out to you on a company let basis! YESS!! This is how success feels like, right? Well, kind of... Do you know what the mistake that most of you had made is? Or at least the mistake that a lot of people make, including myself when starting out – we confirmed the viewing for a few days from now. Even worse – you booked it in for next week!

No! That is not allowed. Never, ever, ever book an appointment for a viewing more than a few days from today. The best time for the viewing is TODAY! NOW! You say to them – "Actually I am in the area within the next 30mins, what is the likelihood we can squeeze a quick 10min appointment? Will be a massive favour if we can do that?". You want to overcommit and over deliver. There is no such thing as under commit and over deliver. You will then say, but if you are actually not in the area in 30mins or you are at work and you cannot do it, or you are just too tired to go. Well, guess what – your letting's agent quite frankly – does not care about that. What they care of is to let out the property as quickly as they can, finding the "most suitable candidate" amongst everyone and get their commission. Your biggest concern should be that you waited for this opportunity for so long – and to be more specific – 157 calls long – and now you are not able to commit to be go to the viewing later today?

I was in this situation before. When I was starting, we were 3x of us that were partnering and were about to start our R2SA business. The problem was that when 2x of us went to view it a few days from now, we then had to get the 3rd person to view it on another day, due to their work schedule. Do you want to know how many deals did we get in the first 4 months? You got that right – ZERO.

To be quite honest here – I did call sick at my work place when I had a few viewings scheduled for the next day. I did prolong my lunch break because I had to drive to the other side of town just to get to the viewing and back (and most LUNCH breaks – the only LUNCH I had was a protein shake as I was not able to have a proper meal whilst rushing to make the appointment). It is your levels of commitment that will determine whether or not you will take a few weeks or a few months to get your 1st deal through.

So just to summarise – once you get to hear those golden words – "Yes we work with other companies as well" – and you know that you have an opportunity to view a property, put an offer and get it to be ran as your 1st Short Term Rental – take it. Ask to view it today, or latest – tomorrow. This way you are putting yourself way ahead of your competition that have other "obstacles" in their way for stopping them from attending that property viewing as early as tomorrow.

Tip #12 – Before & After Photos

If you only knew how important it is to "Document the Journey" you would have started long time ago. Or are you just starting your journey now? Great" Time to document this sh*t!

When you already have got a property that you have just taken from a landlord/agent what is the next steps you need to undertake? Furnish it, right?

Nope, not really. The very first thing you take those keys is for you to take a photo/video of yourself expressing how you feel and what led you to secure this deal and get a hold of those set of keys. More on this later.

After you have the keys – you need to go to the property and take photos/videos of the current condition. You want to make sure that you capture a great "BEFORE" images of "THE BEAUTY" before you transfer it to "THE BEAST" or so called "THE MONEY MAKER".

Capture the full width of each room, take photos of the bathroom, kitchen, garden, hallways – whatever you can and know that once you do a quick "touch up" will make a huge impact and will contrast massively on the "AFTER" photos. And to take the photos of the "bad looking" property, you do not need any fancy/expensive equipment – any phone with a decent camera will work – even them old NOKIAs. Just make sure you can then transfer those photos to your laptop. You don't want them to disappear the same way them phones are slowly disappearing within the early 2020's.

So after you have your 1ˢᵗ set of photos taken. Now you need to get to work and renovate/furnish the property. Fast forward a few days/a few weeks later (depending on how quick you and your team are to renovate and improve the condition/quality of the property) you are ready to take your "AFTER" photos.

Now, very important – you DO NOT want to take them with your NOKIA phone, not even with your IPhone 20+ PRO MAX MEGA PREMIUM LIMITED EDITION. It is not even YOU that needs to take those photos – this is the step that you find yourself a professional property photographer that knows much more about light/shading/angles/proportions etc. when it comes down to photography. You are the professional that knows about property – let the photographer be the one that knows about photography (unless you are a photographer yourself and have all the fancy new tech equipment with you – then fair play to you – you just saved yourself £250 for a photo shoot).

You just guide the photographer of what you want them to focus on when taking those photos, attention to smaller details such as some decorations, or the fact that you offer a DECAF coffee as well (that is a huge benefit to have – will boost your bookings) or whatever you feel the need of having for your "PORTFOLIO PHOTOS" as I like to call them.

Then once the photos are done – there is one last thing you need to do before you pay your photographer – make sure you have your LOGO on either corner on those images – this way now you can use these photos online and have your branding shown and distinguishing yourself from any of your competitor's photos.

And then you pay. And then you are done. You now have your "PORTFOLIO PHOTOS" that you can put on your website/all the travel agencies and show to other estate agents what sort of standard/quality/service you offer to other agents/landlords. This becomes your social proof that you are all about business and service. Plus it makes quite some good content for your socials – those before and after photos combined with some trendy a** music and effects can get you some extra followers on your Only Fans account.

Tip #13 – Take Meter Readings

Are you excited that you just took the keys and now you are ready to get this show going and transform that property to something that you will get 110% monthly occupancy on? Good! Well Done! Before you start though, you need to take a few digits that will save you some headache in the future if you had them earlier than later.

You need to locate your Water, Electricity and Gas (if applicable) Meters. You need to take those meter readings on Day 1. And how I do that and make sure that I do not get mixed up with numbers, dates or properties – I just take a photo of that meter. In your gallery library it will tell you the date/time and location of where the photo was taken. And that is it. And now there are 2x options – if you are a beginner – you save those photos, roll up your sleeves and start working on turning this property around as quickly as you can – remember there are guests waiting for you, even if you have no reservations yet (more on this in the next lesson).

After the property is all ready and you start receiving reservations, then you can worry of setting up your utility providers and giving those meter readings to them. For you guys that are a bit more advanced in this game – as soon as you take those keys and take those photos – send them across to your team and let them set up your monthly payments and submit those meter readings for you – your main priority, of making the property ready in the shortest period of time, does not change.

You must remember that SPEED is very important in this and in any business out there – once you get the keys – you are already losing money. You need to reduce the amount of time you are losing money and start making money by setting up that property as quickly as you can and start receiving payments from your guests. Then worry about all of them monthly bills. The whole A-Z process can be setup within a few weeks from getting hold of those keys.

Tip #14 – Market First!

You have probably heard the saying – "sell the product before you have it"? I certainly did not have that. One of my first UNSUCCESFUL business ideas was to make gym hoodies with motivational quotes on them and sell it to gym rats. Well, I bought a few of them, I made the design, logo, slogan, made the final product, spent a bunch of cash – but never told anyone that I had something to sell.

Then all of the inventory I had, I was not able to sell – hence just gave it to friends and family. I did not know if there is a market for it.

Now let us link this example to your serviced accommodation units. You just got the keys, renovated the property, made it look amazing, took those professional photos and only now you start putting it on those travel agencies and website. That is a big and costly mistake!

What you should have done (as I did not know myself at the beginning) is to create a listing on Airbnb and Booking.com and start promoting your property, before it is ready to be let to your guests.

"WHAT? Are you SERIOUS? How can I have a property that I offer to guests that is not even ready yet? Am I not lying to them? What if they actually reserve it – what do I do then?"

Well, my answer to this is you better get your sleeves rolled up, as those guests are not going to wait for you to take your time and make the property ready for them.

You need to get yourself a deadline. I know it might be difficult at first, especially if this is your first unit, but give yourself some realistic timeframes – for the painting that needs doing (if it does), furniture deliveries, assembly, photos to be taken etc. + adding your personal life circumstances as well (work, family, etc.).

With my very first property we have taken 10x days to turn around from taking the keys to receiving the professional photos. So having at least 2x weeks, depending on the size of the property and number of bedrooms you need to setup. Now we are ready within 2-3 days of taking the keys, but that is because we have systemised it to be so.

Once you have 2x weeks booked in your own calendar, then you need to setup those listings online for your property. For photos – just get 5-7 photos of local landmarks of your own city and upload them – this way you are able to publish and keep your listing active until you receive the ready images from your photographer.

Once your listing is up – you need to go to your Calendar and Availability section and block the next 2x weeks. This means that nobody can reserve with you for those 2x weeks, however any other date after that they can. And this is why knowing that you have a deadline (2x weeks) and knowing that you might be getting a reservation on day 15, by having that urgency in place you will make sure that the property is ready before then. This is how by the time your next monthly rental payment is due – you will have some reservations in/money coming your way to go towards that rental payment and utilities.

So a quick summary – setup your listing first, block your calendar for a few days/weeks ahead and start receiving bookings without wasting any time!

Tip #15 – Internet Is Of The Essence

I might be repeating myself by saying "This is the very first thing that you need to setup once you get the keys for the property", but realistically – these are just the things you need and must setup simultaneously with each other. You need to be having Internet and Wi-Fi connection within your property – and probably this is one of the main things guests will find very frustrated with if you don't have.

The only other problem out there is that – ALL UK broadbands providers are as slow as a herd of asthmatic snails traveling uphill through peanut butter. Yes, they are very slow.

What you need to do to avoid having to deal with poor connection, bad customer service, activation date changes etc is to setup your broadband provider as soon as you know that the deal for this property is going through, your offer is accepted, contracts are signed and you know when you are going to pick up the keys. Time to setup your broadband providers now.

They usually take about 2-4x weeks to send an "engineer" to activate your services. So better be safe than sorry, right?

Another option that is out there is the EE Dongle device that acts like a small router/modem to which you input a SIM card (that you have as Pay as you Go), top it up with 1x months' worth of Internet Data – make sure you change to a Data Package – speak with the cashier where you buy the card from – they will explain how it works. Then you can leave this device and password to the apartment. This way the guests will have Internet/Wi-Fi within the property whilst you are waiting for the broadband provider to wake up and activate their own router.

Then when it is all activated, you make sure that the SIM plan is not on monthly renewable option. After the 1x month runs out, you stop that card and possibly use it once again in the future for your next property (hopefully you do not have to).

Tip #16 – Big Brother Is Watching You!

Is it really a good idea to have security systems in place in your properties or are you just paranoid? Well there is only one way to find out, right?

Leave your apartment unsecured – without knowing how many people go and in and out, not knowing if they smoke inside or not – and you will end up finding your place an absolute wreck! You will see that even you are not that important to be invited to your guest's party that they had organised without letting you know!

Or, you can just put some security measures in place and have a bit more piece of mind. The way we prepare all of our properties is simple – we put a noise detection device in each and one of our properties. The one we use is called Minut. They are very simple to use and install – no need for drilling. You just attach the magnetic plate to the ceiling with the double sided sticker – then charge the Minut module and attach it. Download the app and you are ready to roll – this device can detect – noise, movement, temperature levels, humidity levels, risk of mould. This is a very powerful tool that we started using from the beginning of our journey and has helped us massively to avoid having neighbours complain about the loud noise coming from our property, during the Quiet Hours of the day. Costs about $10-$15pcm for having the subscription + an additional $50 for the device. It is well worth the investment!

The other part of our Big Brother Security Systems that we use is called Blink Camera. Same as the Minut device – it is super easy and simple to install – normally we put the camera outside of our properties, facing the main entrance and detecting who is going in and out. A device is about £90 on Amazon + about $3 monthly subscription for any device up to 3x systems. Anything above that is $10pcm on the Blink Plus Plan.

Having both those devices in each one property that we have save us the trouble of:

-knowing if the cleaners went, cleaned, how long they stayed

-knowing if the guest followed the check-in/check-out times and should you charge them accordingly

-knowing if your guests have invited more people than on the original reservation

-knowing if the guest has smoked in the property

-knowing if the guests have left the heating to the max and left the apartment/house

-knowing if they brought a pet with them and ignored your Animal Policy

-knowing that in any case of an emergency you will be notified no matter what

It is just essential to have this and especially if you want to make sure that you have full control of the situation and then being able to systemise this across the rest of your business.

Tip #17 – Keeping Your Guests Safe

Were you ever in a position that you needed something to prevent a house fire from happening, but you never had the appropriate equipment? That is exactly what we do not want our guests to feel and experience. This is why we equip all of our properties with a Fire Blanket and a small Fire Extinguisher – it costs about £20 for the whole set and you save yourself some of the stress of a guest being a bit clumsy and accidentally attempting to light your property on fire.

Also, we highlight this feature about our property in the online travel agency listings that we advertise. We make sure that there is a photo of them taken as well and included amongst the property photos. We also add this information in the Welcome Pack that we leave in each one of our units. It states where the location of the fire blanket + fire extinguisher is, what is the process of evacuation and assembly point in case of an emergency and informing them that we keep the matter of SAFETY as a high priority.

At the end of the day – if you are using the Rent 2 Rent strategy to have properties let out on Short Term Basis – remember that this property is not even yours – so you need to make sure you are more cautious with what might get wrong and how you can prevent it from happening. Be smart! Tell your guests to be smart! Make money the SAFE way!

Tip #18 – Use Pricing Systems

Have you ever wondered if you are losing money with the nightly rate that you charge your guests? Or you were just not sure how much you need to increase your prices during the summer, how much you need to decrease them during the winter? What about that missed opportunity for those special occasions that you have a special event in your city and everyone else charges 5x what you are and they are getting booked and profiting much much more?

Sadly to say, we lost multiple thousands of pounds over the last few years until we adopted a dynamic pricing system software that we should have used from Day 1. Let me tell you a bit more of how they work. It is a system that integrates with your existing listing on Airbnb Listing or Channel Manager. They compare your property prices with the current market condition, occupancy levels, bookings in advance, average price, etc. and adapt a unique price specifically for your property. Obviously you can change that price if you wish, but your calendar will have different prices every single day. This will allow you to capture the attention to a lot of potential guests and beat your competition by getting that guest reserve with you. You will also be able to manage your minimum nightly stay across your calendar. You might want to have a minimum 2x night stay for the next 7x days, because you would like to fill up the next week with as many bookings as possible.

Remember – every day on your calendar on which you do not have a reservation – you are on a minus on that day. So you want to make sure that within the next 15x days you have high occupancy. However, any day from 90x days from now, you might want to adopt a minimum booking of 5x nights. This will allow you to secure more future revenue by having longer bookings. You can play around with this, but I will be honest – since we added this to our system – we have seen an immediate 2x in average bookings per day.

You don't necessarily need to learn about it in depth – just need to know the basics, but there are quite a few training videos out there of how to use those dynamic pricing tools.

We personally use PriceLabs – it's about $20pcm for having a property on with them, but that $20 you make up super quick by having your prices adapted to your market. There are other tools such as Beyond Pricing and Lodgify.

Tip #19 – WhatsApp For Guests & Cleaning Team

You wondered why the guest left you a bad review. Well this can happen due to multiple reasons – the most common one is – they are d*ckheads. But if we need to delve a bit more into this you are going to find that the guest just wanted some attention from you – they wanted to know how to turn the oven and make a mac and cheese. They were not sure which button they need to press on the remote control to turn the TV on, or they were a little bit disappointed of how the bathroom still smelt of the previous guests. Yukk...

So this is where the "Customer Service" aspect of any business within the Hospitality Industry needs to polish to the T. The way you communicate with your guests and your cleaners is Key!

What we use is direct messing via WhatsApp. The reason for us using that is – you save yourself the hassle and trouble of messaging 20x different guests across 7x different travel agency platforms and loosing track of who is what and where is why. Exactly!

We take our guests from the platform that we they have booked and transfer them across to one direct messaging channel to all of them – WhatsApp. About 98% of our guests have got that app on their phone and the chance of them seeing our messages via that app are much higher than the platform they have reserved on. And the other 2% of them – well, they simply ain't staying with us. Ha-ha – for them we still communicate with them via email + let them know that we are easily reachable via WhatsApp.

Remember – keep it as easy and simple as possible – you need to make their experience hassle free and enjoyable, not overwhelm them with lots of information over the platform they booked in and then forgetting that you have a guest staying in your property, that might have questions that you cannot even answer due to the lack of communication channel between you.

The same thing applies to the cleaners. We set up a group chat with them – there we place all of the information to them – New Reservations/Updates On Reservations/Cleaning Board Updates/Guest Requests/Reporting Damages/Lockbox Code Changes etc.

All of this – through 1x app called WhatsApp. Powerful!

Tip #20 – Taking Direct Bookings – Systemisation

One of the best things in any serviced accommodation business is taking Commission Free Reservations! You can immediately save a 20% on those stays and put that extra cash in your pocket. On a £1,000 reservation you save £200 – that money can go to cover one or a few of your monthly expenses. Or you can use that money to re-invest in the business and promote and market your property even more. The possibilities are limitless.

But how can you get direct bookings and what systems you need to have to achieve that? Well, easiest option is to have a website to which you re-direct your potential guests to. There they can find more information about your place, and reserve it through there – submit their card information – and BOOM. You just got a direct booking. However, let us explore a bit more on where from you can get those direct bookings.

FB groups and Marketplace – having a business page for your business is Essential. Posting regularly on it is a MUST! Not having the time to do it is an EXCUSE. You need to understand that in order for someone to reserve your place – you cannot show them an advert – they open it and they buy it – the principle of going to the Bar, seeing the most beautiful girl out there, going to speak with her and the first thing you ask her is

– come to my place and let's have sex. How many of you would think that this is a bold, but also a stupid move? I mean, I understand – there is still a chance that you can get laid sooner or later by doing that. But at least buy her a drink, talk to her, go on a first date and establish some sort of a relationship. Then you can ask the question you wanted to ask 3x months ago. You chances have increased much more.

Relating back to business – you need to post daily content on you page – educating your followers about what Serviced Accommodation is, the benefits of it etc. Then after they KNOW you, if they still follow you, which means they LIKE you. After that step is done – your next step is for them to TRUST you – and that trust comes from your social proof – your reviews from previous guests, the experience you have provided to your existing clients and how you made them feel. Then your potential guests will become guaranteed guests after they trust of what you and your business is all about. Then you start receiving direct bookings from there.

It is better if you have a Channel Manager in place – the process of collecting their bank information, confirming the booking and sending them an invoice is made very easy.

Lead Generation - do you love spread sheets? Well, whether you do or don't, you'll have to understand that if you do your own lead generation or you hire someone to do it for you, you will need to submit all of that information somewhere and a spread sheet is best because then you can filter the information later. Once you have those Names, Companies in your area, emails and phone numbers – you can start cold calling/sending them emails and introducing them to what you do. You will find out that most people do not want your service – that is normal – but you need that 1x Construction Company or Recruitment Agency or whoever else that has constant inflow of people in your town for short term and they usually stay at hotels. Perfect – now it is your chance to schedule a meeting with them – discuss how you can help them and close the deal.

Previous Guests – it is really important to build your database of your previous guests – names, phone numbers, emails etc. This is how you can bring them back to your property in the future and you can even offer them a small discount (lower than the 20% normally taken from the travel agencies) and they will still be happy to take it. You need to have made a good impression and left them with a positive experience since the first time they stayed with you.

So a recap on Direct Bookings – get in front of previous guests – new potential guests by using lead generation and social media advertising. Once you start getting positive feedback from them and interest in them reserving with you – then either do it yourself via a Channel Manager or manually block your calendars on the travel agencies, and send your guest the necessary forms to complete, sign and take payment. We get our Virtual Assistant to take of all of this – and you should too!

Tip #21 – Receiving Payments / Payment Merchants

If you are listing your properties with Airbnb, Booking.com, VRBO, Trivago and all of the rest of those travel agencies, you will not necessarily need to have a payment merchant, because they will be able to automatically take care of the payments and pay-outs to you. What is the reason then for having a Payment Merchant? Well, glad you asked!

When you have a website where you promote your properties you would like to have some type of software that safely and securely takes payments from your guests. Also you would like to pay as little as possible for those transactions to happen. And most importantly you want your guest's money to come to your pocket ASAP, right?

This is exactly why you must have a payment merchant! There are hundreds of options out there most trusted are PayPal, First Data (nowadays called Clover), Stripe, GoCardless, Ayden and many more. I personally use First Data.

What happens is, when you already have a Channel Manager, and then you get yourself hooked up with one of them Payment Merchants. Voila! Now, payments that come from most travel agencies, including Booking.com, you will be able to receive the guest's card information automatically. Then you will be able to pre-authorise, charge and refund cards. And money is send to you within a few days. If you wait on Booking.com – it will take 15 days to a month. Now that will mess up your cash flow massively.

One last reason for having a payment merchant is this – if all else fails – and you need to take payment from your guest, but you do not do cash – you must have a plan B to be able to take those payments somehow. And best thing is – you will be able to take all of the different debit, credit, coupon, benefit cards out there – Visa, Debit, Credit, MasterCard, JBL, Maestro, AMEX etc.

Get yourself a payment merchant as soon as you can – it will save you time and money in the long run! A small bonus I would like to that is – the easier it is to open an account with a Payment Merchant – usually the higher they will charge you per transaction and vice versa. Try open a PayPal account – takes minutes. I remember when I opened my First Data account it took me 2.5 weeks + someone had to come to my office (my bedroom) to take photos of my workplace and office + see what type of company equipment (laptop + mouse) I was using. Ridiculous, right? But I got very good rates because of how difficult it was to open. Keep that in mind when you go for yours!

Tip #22 – Charging The Guest For Extras?

Have you ever wondered why hotels make so much money? Well, one of the main reasons is because of the sh*t ton of marketing they do and the amount of variables that go in running a hotel business – restaurants, swimming pools, events, shows, casinos, etc. They do not only rely on room rentals. The secret is in the pudding as they say – the big hotel chains rely on Upsells.

What is an Upsell? Simply said – an upsell is something that you sell as a bonus/extra in addition to the main purchase (in this case the room they are selling). So what could be an upsell within the hotel business? Charging extra for Wi-Fi? Pay for Parking at the hotel? Paying extra for Breakfast? The list just goes on and on. But this is exactly why a hotel that is an established brand is a money making machine – Upsell!

Now let us transfer this into our Short Term Rental business – what can you upsell? Well if you charge for Wi-Fi and parking it will be a bit too much for a guest to choose you rather than the 2x cheaper hotel right next door, wouldn't it? So, what we currently do, and have been doing since day one is – charging extra for additional guests, additional weekly cleaning, early check-ins and late check-outs, transport services, having a premium or a platinum gift packs (leave a basket of goodies to your guests – some fresh groceries, bottle of wine, fruits and veg, etc). Let's break it down

-additional guests – if you have a 1x bed flat that can accommodate 4x guests – has a sofa bed in the living room that converts to a bed where 2x people can easily sleep – we have our normal rate for up to 2x guests. Then we charge additional £10 - £25 per guest – depending on the season. So as an example – if 4x people reserve – instead of them paying £100 for example, they will be paying £150 (£100 for the first 2x guests and then 2 x £25). Doing this you can maximise your property by not doing much.

-additional weekly cleans – if you have a guest that is staying at your property for let's say 14x nights, you would like to offer them a change of linen + midweek clean wouldn't you? But then telling them that they need to pay for it – most of the time they would not want to, which is quite understandable. How we deal with that is simple – we just add the extra weekly cleaning within the reservation price for the guest and don't tell them –

then we say that we are offering a free midweek clean and they are happy because they do not need to pay for it. It is the old trick with £50 only today – nobody buys – you put another sign with the "old price" saying £100 and it is crossed out and below you have the "new" price of £50 and everyone is happy to pay for that. It is the same analogy.

-early check-ins and check-outs – most of the time the guest would ask for them to check-in a bit earlier or check-out a bit later – and the more flexible you are with them the better the review they will leave you with. However, keep this in mind, if you offer it for free, you are messing your Cleaner's schedule and leaving them with less time to clean that specific property for + if you have a few properties in the area that you have accepted free early check-ins and late check-outs, your cleaners will be rushing to clean them before the new guests arrive which will eventually compromise on the quality and the future reviews that you will get + your cleaners can get annoyed and leave you. So how do you compensate for that – well, it is simple – charge the guests extra. An additional £10 - £15 for a flexible timing might reduce the guest's enquires about that, but also increases your profitability from the ones that do not mind spending the extra cash. Then to be fair with your cleaners – you give part of that money to them, so they are happy as well.

And now it is a Win-Win-Win scenario. This is how you generate extra money for no extra "time".

-transport services – you can offer airport/train station/coach station/cruise ship pickup options to your guests - you can speak with a family member, friend or whoever you know that drives and is happy to make some extra cash to the side. Tell them that occasionally you might be getting a guest enquiring for transport services to the property and if they are happy they can get a percentage of that cash – say you do a 50/50 split with them. This is another Win-Win-Win scenario where everyone benefits.

-premium goodie bags – you know the hotel "all inclusive" or "breakfast included" room package they offer. Well, we are not far off from it here in the Serviced Accommodation business as well. You can have that included in your description online, have photos taken of the different baskets and what you offer. Then if a guest reserves the premium goodie basket – your cleaner simply goes to the shop, buys all of those stuff, leaves them at the property and the guest does not have to worry to go to the shop when they arrive. An example of this is: Your premium goodie basket offers – wine, bread, ham, cheese, water, eggs, sweets – this costs you £10. Your guest pays you £20. You give £5 to your cleaner and you keep £5. All sorted once again. You can choose whatever you'd like. Just be mindful and make sure that the products you include – the guest is aware, because the last thing that you want is your guest getting an allergic reaction to that, being sent to the hospital and then suing you afterwards. Plus on top of everything – leaving you a bad review – that is just unforgivable!

So to sum it up – you can add extras to upsell to your guests and they will be more than happy to pay and have a great experience in your property.

Tip #23 – When To Pay Your Cleaners

You ever wondered when should your cleaners be paid? If at all?

Normally what we have done is setup our payments towards the cleaning team on the last Friday of every month. This way they know that you have all of your total monthly cleanings accounted for and you are not under/over paying them.

Now there are options where you could possibly be paying them once every cleaning was done – but then that is a complete hassle, because of the amount of invoice you need to deal with and time taken to make payments. Plus, it affects your day to day cash flow. We do the payment once a month, on a one single invoice and it takes a minute or less to count up the reservations and amount payable and transfer that across after cross referencing with the invoice. It is done. Until next month.

Try and systemise that and communicate thoroughly with your cleaners – at the end of the day – they are people – they need money as well. So if you have – let's say during halfway of the month, they want an advance on their check – pay them, be a human. Just make sure to monitor this of how often it happens and why.

Another thing to keep in mind is the quality of each clean once done. If you pay them after every cleaning is done – possibly they might be more motivated to work for you as they get money on the day. Whereas if you pay them once a month, their quality might decline as they have not seen a single penny drop in their account from you for the past 29 days, hence the quality of the cleaning can possibly drop. This is all subjective and depends on the person you are dealing with. But try to stay on top of these things. It will save you energy on dealing with guests that leave negative reviews due to poor cleaning standards.

Tip #24 – Keep Your SA Smelling Nice

Have you ever been to a hotel room where you can just feel that stench of filth throughout your skin, nose, ears and all of your 6 senses come together in a complete disgust. Arghhhh.

No! Do not allow that feeling to ever enter in any of your guest's mind! Make sure that after every cleaning is done – your cleaning team sprays some Airwick, some nice tropical fruit juice aroma in the air. Those Caribbean coconut, mango, lemon, kiwi scent that will create another atmosphere within your property. It will take your guest physically and mentally to the destination of their dreams – on that golden sandy beach with the light breeze of air in their hair, sun shining on their skin, waves crashing on the beach, surfers avoiding their daily dose of death threats with the sharks chasing them to the beach shore and the playful music of a beach drummer that just graduated from university but decided he will live his dream and become a beach drummer in the Caribbean beaches. Even though they just entered your property in the rainy and sad atmosphere of the London suburbs.

So to keep this short and sweet – you can leave a spray in the property for your cleaners to spray before they leave (after they are done cleaning) or you can have those electrical aroma dispensers that you put in the socket and release the smell of cleanliness in the air. Or just leave them with a car freshener – whichever works best for you really. Let's be honest – do not leave them with a car freshener – EVER. Only if you offer it within your premium goodie basket.

Tip #25 – Get Rid Of The Stench Of Cigarettes

Do you smoke? If you don't – well done to you!! Smoking is a bad habit to have! However, if you do smoke – how could you blame your guests from smoking? It does not seem fair, does it?

Of course it isn't fair. Especially if they have broken your "house rules" that clearly states – NO SMOKING INSIDE THE PROPERTY! Does that mean that your guests skipped English classes and went to hang out with the "cool kids" back in school?

Honestly, that is 0% of your concern. What you need to focus now is getting rid of the stench that overwhelms the whole property – even the bathroom!

The best way to do it is to have a handy lil device called Ozone Machine Generator. Cost about £70 on Amazon, but it is a life saviour. What this does is it breaks down the O2 molecules in the air (hence it is a bit dangerous) and this way it eliminates the smell of cigarettes and any other bad smell within your rental property.

What you need to do is to close all windows and doors, turn the machine on and leave for about 30-45mins at least. This will be sufficient enough time for it to eliminate the bad smell in the air. What your cleaners can do is – leave the machine – go and clean another property, or grab a coffee whilst the air gets "purified" (because you do not want them to be inside whilst this dangerous lil fella is doing its thing). Then they come back, stop the machine, open all doors and windows – clean the property, spray with some nice tropical spray and your SA is as good as gold!

Also on top of getting this problem solved – you can charge your guest on their damage deposit. They did not follow your rules, so now it is time for you to take back what is rightfully yours.

Tip #26 – Secure The Damage Deposit First

You just received a reservation. You are happy! The guest just messaged – wanting to cancel! You are sad!?

Have you ever been in these types of situations? Where someone "accidentally" booked your property and now they want to cancel and your Cancellation Policy is Fully Flexible and they can get all their money back?

We are not going to talk about how you can undergo a mental therapy due to stressful situations like this. I will tell how you need to secure your damage deposit first, so that you don't have to chase it from the guest when it is a little too late.

Most travel agencies out there (excluding Airbnb) – it is the hosts (your) responsibility to handle and deal with the damage/security deposit. This money is normally withhold from your part as a host as a reassurance that your guests will respect and not make any damaged to your place. After they check out and upon full inspection from you/your team you must send full/partially the damage deposit back. If at all.

So when you receive a reservation from a guest – you need to make sure that within the platform you have advertised – it clearly states that you are charging a damage deposit + how much.

Now most guest don't read that fine print – so they wouldn't even notice – until a £300+ is pending on their bank and they start chasing you up for you to refund that money back.

So the way I prefer to do it (you can choose whichever option works best for you), is this – I collect automatically payment for the reservation (this includes reservation fee + cleaning fee) and then 1x day prior their arrival we have an automatic pre-authorisation within our Channel Manager system to "freeze" the damage deposit from the guest's account. Normally there are 2x outcomes of this:

-1st – the guest has enough funds and you are able to successfully pre-authorise their card – that means that when they check-out – if there are any damages – you just take that payment. If there isn't – you cancel the pre-authorisation and that money gets "released" back into their account

-2nd – the guest has insufficient funds – meaning that you are not able to pre-authorise the damage deposit. Now in this case you have to choose – you can communicate with your guest to get another card from which you can pre-authorise the damage deposit, or they pay it in another way (bank transfer, cash, crypto, OnlyFans subscription – whichever one works best for you). If they are not happy to do that – you have the full right to contact the travel agency from which they have reserved from and cancel their reservation – as they, once again, did not follow your policies and house rules – as pre-approved – you are eligible and entitled to pre-authorise their damage deposit before their stay.

Now, when I started out, I never knew what a damage deposit is – I never charged one, and when I needed to get some compensation from the guest after they threw down a party to which I was never invited or broke a few glasses and a few TVs, they were nowhere to be founds + the travel agencies will turn around and say "it was your responsibility as a host to take a damage deposit from your guest prior to their arrival". Lesson learnt the hard way.

So to sum this up – always, pre-authorise a damage deposit, explain to the guest that this will happen – so that they don't call you 2am asking why did you take more money from them than necessary (been there) and try and avoid taking cash as a damage deposit – it is just inefficient if you are trying to grow and expand a short term rental business.

Tip #27 – Know Your Cancellation Policies

I was struggling with this a lot. Is it fully flexible, flexible, moderate, strict, super strict, ultra strict...? I was just hearing BS after BS... it was all the same to me!

However, realising what the difference is and what cancellation policy guests are keen on having for them as a backup plan if they want to cancel your property – you need to know what the differences are.

Now let us start with Strict Cancellation Policy. Anything from Strict to Ultra Mega Hyper Strict means that if a guest decides to make a cancellation with you – their money that they will be paying or have already pay will (in most cases) not be refunded back to them. Only the cleaning fee is what they will receive back. This way you are in full control of your calendar and cash flow. Yes, you will get most guests come up with a BS excuse that they need the money refunded back to them even though you are not obliged to do that under your Strict Cancellation Policy. It is in your hands whether or not you send them the money back.

Now, keep this in mind – some of their reasons might be fair and reasonable – a family member passed away – their plane tickets got cancelled, etc. So in some cases you can refund them their money back. However, at the end of the day, you are running a business, not a charity – so if someone has made a reservation with you and their check-in is tomorrow and they cancel – what is the likelihood of someone else reserving tomorrow – pretty low. So I personally would keep their reservation fee, refund them the cleaning fee and move on. Another scenario may be – if they made a reservation after 3x months and they want to cancel – in this case (most of the time

I will still keep the cash), however you have those dates – 3x months in the future – to worry about filling them in. So it is not that bad – you can get a guest to pay you more or reserve for longer – so it is not necessarily a big loss. So just be mindful that when you using any Strict Policy – you are in full control of keeping that money.

Let us look into the Flexible Cancellation Policy. Now, a lot of the travel agencies out there would recommend you use this policy as a default – they will say to you that a lot more guests prefer to reserve an accommodation that offers some sort of Flexible Cancellation Policy – which they are absolutely right about. But it puts you and your business and cash flow in a lot of uncertainty. The guest can cancel within a window of a specific number of days (depending on which type of Flexible Cancellation Policy you choose from), and get their full refund back. This way your calendar might be looking full and you might be having 100% occupancy rates, but with the likelihood of every single guest of cancelling and getting all of their money back and leaving you with nothing. The problem in this situation is that you still have bills to pay and you need to come up with that money somehow.

Look into this scenario as an example – you have 10x guests reserved for 3x nights each one of them – covering a complete 30/30 (100%) occupancy in your calendar. Simple maths right.

Now they are all on the Flexible Cancellation Policy. Now the first guest decides to cancel – the one that is meant to check-in tomorrow. So they just receive their full money back and leave you with a 3x day gap. The problem is that during the different months and the different seasons, guests have a different "booking window" every single time. For example – in the summer months you might see guests booking 30 – 40 – 50 days in advance. This means that, if we are in June, you are already getting reservations for July and August – which is great news. But some months you might be having shorter booking windows such as – 5 -10 -15 days – which means that guests are not interested in reserving far in advance do to multiple factors.

So, relating back to the scenario from above – if you are now to be having those 3x night bookings – the people that are looking for an accommodation today for tomorrow are very few – they are looking a few weeks ahead already. So this leaves you with 27/30 reserved nights right. Now 3x days past and next guest is meant to check-in, but guess what – he is on Flexible Policy and he cancels. So now you have another 3x day's gap. And this repeats itself until end of the month you have probably had 2x or 3x guests that have stayed out of 10x and you lost massively on revenue. Thanks only to your Flexible Cancellation Policy.

Now let us compare – there is no right or wrong answer here – you choose whichever one works best for you – in some winter months that your occupancy is low, you might want to keep you cancellation policy open and flexible and try and squeeze a few more bookings in even with having the chances of them cancelling, you can still make a few more bucks out of them, than not having any bookings, because your policy is strict. So it all depends.

Adapt to your markets, follow trends and observe what your competitors are doing. You will know what to do when the shift happens.

Tip #28 – Systemise Your Maintenance Drills

You need to understand that when starting with any business – you will have to work in the business – you will have to get your hands dirty if you would like to 1st understand how much effort and work it takes to perform a task and 2nd save money. The number one biggest reason why businesses fail is the Negative Cash flow – this is when you are getting less money than you expend eventually leading to you shutting down your business and declaring bankruptcy.

Now how does this relate to Tip #28? Well, in order to systemise anything within a business you need to understand what is the safest, least expensive, productive and efficient method to do a task. If we take Maintenance for example – you need to have a few things in place: know a bunch of maintenance people, understand what possible damages might happen within your property, make sure you have funds in your account (ideally you must have a credit card), or possibly be able to charge the guests for any problem that has occurred within the property due to their negligence whilst they stay with you.

The way we do things is this – a guest reports a maintenance problem. We class it as a Low, Moderate or High Risk. Anything that is a high risk gets dealt with it immediately – our team send messages to all of our Maintenance people we know (that are capable of sorting this problem out), we see who is available to come as soon as possible. Then they come to the property – we send him our already made up information about the address to him and depending on whether or not the guest will be in or not, we contact the maintenance person with the guest. After problem is solved, maintenance person communicates back with us, sends us the invoice, we pay it same day and save the invoice to our files.

Now with the Moderate Risk issue – we assess it how bad it is, can the guest live with it (if they are checking out tomorrow and the lighbulb in the corridor stopped working – is it really essential for us to send someone, pay them £100 for changing the lighbulb? Maybe not. So we need to understand what the situation is and act accordingly. We still communicate with our maintenance people and schedule them in after the guest has left – this way they will have an easier entry.

With Low Risk issues we put them on a list, wait until a few of them build up and then send the maintenance person to fix them in one go, rather than sending him a few times (will cost more if you send them there a few times for small things).

So what about when the cleaner goes to clean and finds something that needs fixing – well, it is the same situation – she messages our group chat – the team picks up on it – asses if this is a Low, Moderate or High Risk and transfer it across to the maintenance people (to which I have access to as well – want to make sure that our maintenance people treat my team with respect!

To sum it up – make sure you use the tools that are available for everyone out there – phones, WhatsApp, Google, Lockboxes etc. Anything that you can put in place, connect the right people and you just sit down and observe how the problems get fixed. You just have to pay in the end. Possibly.

Tip #29 – Choose The Right Tradesmen For The Job

You have got a plumbing issue in your property and a carpenter comes to the rescue… Not ideal, is it? But I have been there myself – getting people with 0% skills and qualifications in a specific field to do a job they never have the first place. Worst of all is – they want the same money to be paid to them as if they were that trade's person. Never again!

How do you choose them then? Well it all depends where you find your trades professionals. There are multiple websites out there such as checkatrade, mybuilder etc that you can post an advert for free – express what type of problem you need help with and then your phone will start buzzing with messages and phone calls from interested tradespeople.

After you have checked their profile – you can see previous jobs they have then, previous reviews from other customers and assess if this is the right person for the job. Then when you call them you will get a gut feeling based on their talking to you, how busy they are, how many people they have under them as a team or is it just themselves, how many years of experience etc. Then you can possibly schedule them for the job.

The best thing to do is to test and trial them out. Give them small jobs – see how well they perform, do they turn up on time, are they reliable, do they clean up after themselves etc. Based on those things you can possibly start pushing and giving them bigger and better tasks for them that take longer time to do and they get more money out of it. But you need to establish respect and authority – you are the client, you want the job done to a specific standard – if they cannot do it, you move onto the next one (obviously don't be d*ckheads about it, but within reason).

So a recap on this – put adverts out , get tradespeople to contact you, filter them out based on a conversation/availability/experience levels/reviews, give them small tasks, filter them even more, establish relationships, build a good and reliable team of trades professionals.

Tip #30 – Filter & Expand Your Power Team

So this one relates back to Tip #29 – the more people you introduce to your business (giving them a trial to do a task or work for you within that business), the more you will be able to filter them out and leave the big and the best that will form the foundation of your Power Team.

Now what type of people is it that you need within your Power Team? Well, it all depends on the industry you are in. To keep it short and tidy – we are talking about the Rent to Rent Serviced Accommodation sphere. So, these are the main key players that you need and I will explain why they are needed for:

-lettings agents

-maintenance people

-cleaners

-virtual assistant/business partner

-investors

-solicitor

Lettings Agents – well, you need a property don't you. What is the best one to find one? Directly through a Landlord is what most of you might say. Yes, you are probably right. However, a

Landlord might have only a few properties under their belt, whereas a lettings agent will be getting hundreds of deals in front of them every single week. So, if you want to make sure that you have constant flow of deals coming your way – make good relationships with your local lettings agents, view some properties, get a few deals with them. Next time something comes their way, who do you think will be the next person they contact to show them that property? Exactly, do not limit yourself to Landlords only.

Maintenance People –the maintenance people you gather as a team are 1/3 of any short term rental business. Now I understand that you cannot guarantee your maintenance guy constant work from the get-go. However, if you would like to grow this business and not treat it as a hobby, you can prove to your maintenance people that you are in the process of acquiring more and more properties. If they enjoy working for you, they will be happy to know that you can supply them with more and more business, hence you can rely more on them eventually. Solidify your 1/3 of your serviced accommodation business by getting the right maintenance people in place from day 1.

Cleaners – the cleaning team is the other 1/3 of any short term rental business. You need to establish a good relationship with either a cleaning company or individual cleaners that are able to help you with the whole jazz of cleaning the property, re-stocking the inventory, washing, drying, ironing etc. You can find them online – Facebook groups (mothers that have children that need to drop them at school at 9am and pick them up before 3pm – which is the ideal time for them to clean your properties), Google them (find local companies that operate in doing the whole A-Z process for you), speak with your friends (they might know someone that is looking for that type of part time job). Remember to give adequate instructions from day 1 to your cleaning team – the way they start cleaning is the way they will carry on, so you want to make sure that they understand how much Quality means to you and your business. Lastly, don't forget to reward them. For good and positive reviews – guests that say that the cleaning was done to an amazing standard, and it was fresh and tidy – give bonuses out – don't be a greedy lil b*tch.

Virtual Assistant/Business Partner – this is the last 1/3 of the structure for any good serviced accommodation business to run smoothly and operate effectively. The communication with the guests, cleaners, maintenance people, tracking payments, extra requests from guests – all of that – your virtual assistant can do – for a fraction of the price. I live in the UK and am talking about hiring Virtual Assistants from outside the UK – mostly people living in Asia. The main reason is this – price and effectiveness. They can perform those tasks that you don't want to for $3-$5 per hour. Which is basically nothing, when you have plans to scale and grow?

Also, they are very respectful and reliable (at least the people that work on my team). I have put down Business Partner to this as well – if you have a business partner that is interested and driven the same way that you are – your business has no boundaries of growth. They can be out there doing viewings, whilst you are setting up another property, or they can be dealing with maintenance people whilst you are taking payments from guests. Having a business partner is a must! I started solo, but a few years later I realised the benefit of having someone on your team that is there to support you in all aspects of that business. Find yourself one as well!

Investors – you want to grow, but you need money? And you don't have it? So you stop?!

Read that again. Now go in the bathroom, splash some cold water on your face and slap yourself. Do you think that the lack of money should stop you from achieving your dreams and building something for future generations to come? NO!

I do not advise you to get money from everyone and anyone, no. I am just saying that getting an investor on board, someone that can passively sit on the other side, throw some cash at you and get a return on their investment, whilst you grind it out and grow your business. Notably to say, I did not start with having an investor. Not until my 3rd property – 1.5 years into me being in the game. It was a 9x bed / 9x bath HMO (House of Multiple Occupation) or as some people call it Share House. It is a slightly different strategy than Serviced Accommodation, but hey ho – I had to try everything right! So, the problem was that with this one, if all rooms were empty, I had to pay £4,000+ in expenses each month if I was to take this beast by myself.

By having an investor that you join forces and become business partners – now my liability is halved. I do not have the carry the burden of that £4,000+ by myself, but that also does not mean that I am planning to. Plan was to make profit – and that is what we did – 1.5x years later still pushing having that unit and it is preforming as a GEM! But that is all thanks to me getting an Investor that was able to help me grow. As the saying goes "Better have 50% of something, than 100% of nothing!"

Solicitor – having a good solicitor means that you can reduce paying lots of TAX! Yes, you've heard it from me. If you are solicitor is telling you at the end of your financial year that this is how much tax you need to pay etc – in my books – they are fired! Their job is to make sure that they structure your business expenses in a way that help your business, rather than bring it down. I am not going to lie though, it is difficult to find a competent solicitor nowadays.

If you were to get a big firm to track your accounts and you have difficulty to get a hold of them when needed. That is a red flag. This does not mean that I can get a hold of my solicitor every time I call her – maybe on a Sunday night at about midnight – but still, you need to have clear communication with your solicitor – both of you have to be on the same page, literally, of how the last year looked like for your business, what can be done to make sure that you structure your business for the next year and pay less tax, whilst making more money (I am not a financial advisor, and if you are the taxman reading this – I am glad you are reading a book of how to run a short term rental business, you have finally escaped the Matrix).

Tip #31 – Get Compliant Before Getting Sued

I used to believe that "Getting my ducks in a row" was how any business should start off. I was wrong. As my mentor once said – this is called "positive procrastination" – I was putting actions steps that I thought were necessary, before I was out there doing the viewings and getting the deals!

So, linking it back to Tip #31, getting compliant is not your 1st step in this business. But is also definitely not your last. What I mean by that is this – you should not be worrying about which type of business liability insurance or public indemnity you should be choosing – is it the one that covers you up to £1mil or £10mil? Complete nonsense!

Your main worry needs to be is to get the property to start paying you MONEY first and then you can focus on getting your business insurance in place. You definitely want to have insurances there in case if you are being sued by a guest, landlord, agent etc. But you are less likely to get sued if you don't have a property in the first place.

So summing this up – get your deal first, get some money coming in, then pay for those insurances and compliances, then go out and get more properties that will bring more money in! That's the name of the game!

Tip #32 – Inspect After Your Cleaner

How much do you trust your cleaners? Do you just pay them and hope they have done a good job, and then you wait to receive a negative review from your guest of how dirty the whole property was. Then you tell your cleaner off? A little too late, don't you think?

There are a few ways to understand and track if your cleaning team has done a good job, before your guest has checked in. Ready for it?

First, you want to understand how long they have stayed within the property. The way to do that is to have a security camera outside of your property – a one that you have access to from your phone – you can use Blink or Ring. This will detect when the cleaner enters and exits the property. If some of you are paying your cleaner per hour (which I personally go against), at least you know if they are lying to you about the time they have stayed in. Knowing how long your cleaner has been there – problem solved.

Secondly, you want to see if they have used the hoover inside the property, but you forgot to put a camera inside the apartment – ahh sh*t. Or wait, is that the only way? Nope! Remember about the Minut device I mentioned in Tip #16? Exactly – you can track the noise levels within the property for the period of time your cleaner has been there. And guess what – when a hoover/vacuum cleaner has been put on, your Minut Noise Device detects those higher decibels in the air and notifies you that the hoover has been on for this amount of time. So, hoover has been on – checked.

Another thing we tend to do is give out a checklist – things that they need to do – and every time they finish, they take a photo of it and send it to us (our cleaning group chat that we have over WhatsApp). Now, you might say okay, what if they just write it down but don't actually do the things they are meant to on that checklist – well, then we ask them to send us a video of the apartment after it is cleaned (now, we would only ask this at the beginning, after you establish good trust and relationship with them, you can reduce the amount of checks you do with them, but still stay diligent about your processes). Also, as a final precaution/measure, someone from the team will do spontaneous visits – before, during and after the cleaner has left. To check how everything is going, are they running on good schedule, are they marking the checklist as appropriate. Just making sure that all runs smoothly.

You might think that only a control freak will do this – well let me tell you this – if you are not a control freak of your own life and the way you run your business – you would never build solid foundations from which the upper layers of that building will be built. You need to establish that structure to the business where your team will follow and go through the clear path you have set them on to.

Tip #33 – What To Do With The Food In The Fridge

Take it home and share it with your family! I ain't joking. As funny as it sounds, this is the reality sometimes. You will have guests leave food in the fridge, you will find an unprepared English breakfast there (unopened can of beans, some eggs on the shelf, bit of bacon in a pack...), so what do you do in this case – you PREPARE that English Breakfast.

Getting off track. Honestly, with the food that is left there you have some options available of what to do with it. One option is to throw it away. Now, it is a sin throwing food away, but if it is a last bite of a pizza or 28ml of orange juice – that is acceptable. The other option is to get your cleaner to collect the good food and leave it with your local beggar, the person that is on the street (most of the time right next to the local supermarkets), and do something good for them (don't give them money for them to go and buy drugs), give them food so that they have a meal for the day. Also, another option that we have is to get the cleaner to take that unopened food for her and her family. Food is food at the end of the day, so if them getting food is considered a small bonus/gesture from us to them, then be it.

But make sure that you don't leave any food from previous guests to the new guests, that is just not allowed. Unless, you offer breakfast plans with your stay, or hampers that you give out and prepare for them upon their arrival/check-in.

Tip #34 – How To Deal With No Parking?

I will be honest here – it is quite difficult to find a good property in a central location that will have an allocated parking space – very rare. However, realise that because your property does not have that available parking space, you are not going to be getting guests staying with you.

How many times have you stayed in a hotel and they charged you for parking – which again, it was quite of bit of cash per day just to leave your car outside. This is called "a legal robbery". Now, what you can do – as in previous examples – you have a few options. You can speak with your next door neighbour – if you can use their parking space (let's say they don't have a car and don't drive and they are interested in making some cash from you by utilising that parking space). Done deal, you just rented your neighbours parking space, your guests can park there, and everyone is happy.

Now what about if your neighbour does not like you – then it'll be a bit more difficult to rent his parking space, don't you agree? The second option that we have available is to offer the guest the closest street or multi-storey car parking. This way by you telling them how far away it is from your property, how much it will cost them, telling them how secure that is and how the area is like at night – you are keeping your doors still open for the "potential" guest to become an "actual" guest. You tell them how much it is, give them all the information to them and it is up to them to decide. What you don't do is tell them "sorry, but we don't have parking". They will never reserve with you.

As a host, your job is to make sure that your guest gets as much information as they need from you, and you providing them with a great experience at the end of the day. This is how you increase your chances of getting more reservations even if you don't offer a parking space at your own property.

Tip #35 – Nosy Neighbours

Please tell me you have them as well. You are in the midst of setting up your property that you will be letting out to random guests, and your neighbour stands there, pretending they are not watching you, but believe me ... they are watching. And they are not only watching, they are taking notes (who are you, why you having so much furniture going into that small studio apartment, why are they getting that pink paint in there, why do they need so much fake plants and decorations in there, why is that camera that they are installing outside of the property overlooks their property – are you the person that is spying on them now?).

They will be having so many so many questions, and the fact that they cannot do much until your guests throw a party to which you wouldn't even be invited to, and the police gets called and your agent gives you a 1 month notice, what an experience that would be, eh?

Now, remember – the more friends you make within the business the better for your future growth. If you introduce yourself to your neighbours, greet them every time you go passed your property, and leave a good impression – then they will not be against you. You will have a local "ally" that can be your eyes and ears when your security systems fail.

So don't always think that your neighbours are there to hate on you. You will get that odd Karen's out there that is without a doubt. But try and understand that if that is your property to be doing business with people, then their property is the place they call home. So it is absolutely normal to be weary of who is the "new kid on the block". Make sure that that "new kid" is actually a good person.

Tip #36 – Find An Investor – Passive & Active JVAs

I have touched on this topic earlier – finding investors within any business and particularly in Property Investing it is crucial. You have only 3x things that you can offer to anybody – knowledge, time and money. If you don't have the money, but have the time and knowledge, you can join forces with someone that does not have the time or knowledge, or even the geographical location that you have to be doing business there, but is more than happy to lend you some cash, lean back and watch his ROI (return on investment) get paid back with a good interest. This is what is called a Passive Investor. They are happy to lend money against a project, idea, business that has a positive return of cash based on the market research (knowledge/skill) that you have done and the work (time/energy) that you are willing to offer in exchange for that partnership.

An Active Investor is something different. This is when you have someone that is actively involved in the business opportunity that you offer them. They can be lending cash but also wants to actively work within that business. This is where, for example, they lend you cash for the next property deal, but you show and train them how the process works, then they do it themselves (they get to understand it and find out if this is something they enjoy doing or would they just want to sit back and let you do all the work).

I have had a few passive investors that have just lend over cash and were happy to get a return on their investment. This in one way was great for me as there wasn't anyone there to tell me how to operate my business. However, if you do need the support of that someone, you will only find it in an Active Investor – someone that is happy to learn or even better – they have been there themselves, they just want to expand in your geographical location let's say and they give you all the support and knowledge they can so that they can make this partnership/investment worthwhile for both of you.

So if you ask me which one is better – my answer will be BOTH. Get yourself some Passive Investors that are not in your way when you are in the process of building your business, but also have an Active Investor out there that you can learn from yourself or leverage their time as well.

Tip #37 – Last Minute Bookings

Love them or hate them, just don't disregard them. One of my first bookings that I had when I started with my first rental was a reservation (today for today), which was first red flag. I already had the linen setup for 1x guest that was meant to check-in tomorrow and at 8pm at night we received this 1x night booking for 4x guests. By the time I was about to call Booking.com to cancel it, I received a phone call from the guest asking how can they check-in. Myself panicking, because it was my very first experience in dealing with this type of situation I told the guest that we had no hot water and we would have to cancel the reservation. They said they will not be showering, just sleep and take the morning train back to London, it was 2x girls and 2x boys (another obvious red flag), that just came to visit their parents and were off the next morning.

So, Nick being Nick, understanding their situation gave them the code for the lockbox. That was where the damage was done! I did not have any security systems in place from the beginning. So I did not what was happening in that property. Until the next morning when the cleaner came in to check – she called me and told me the "good news" – the apartment was still there... but they have thrown a wild party – balloons, liquor spillages everywhere, vomit all over the bed, blocked shower cabin and on and on. And the best thing of all – the new guest was checking-in after less than 3x hours for a 15x night stay.

We have sorted it all out, cleaner cleaned to the best of her ability, the guest was happy when he came in. But the lesson taken from this, still stings till this day. Ever since that happened, we have implemented a 24x hour block out period (meaning that the earliest reservation a guest can make is at least 24x hours from now – which will give us enough time to prepare the property for the right number of guests etc.). We also are able to charge a higher amount for closer to the day bookings, if we feel that the likelihood of having "dodgy" guests is high.

So, when you are thinking of the Last Minute Bookings – don't treat them with fear (make sure you've got your security systems in place) and don't be afraid to charge more. Every day that your calendar is empty is you losing money. Do not compromise on the risk of getting your property wrecked, but consider the positives against the negatives and decide how you would prepare for your Last Minute Bookings.

Tip #38 – Single Night Bookings – Should You Avoid Them?

Did you read my last tip? What do you think my opinion is then?

I will be weary to allow 1x night bookings due to the very first reservation we got that did not go so well. But this does not mean that you should not allow them. It all depends on how certain you are that you will attract the "right people" into your property – if your prices are very low and you allow 1x nighters, best of luck to you my friend.

There is this debate of having a low occupancy of bookings across a month is very bad, to having a high occupancy, which means you are "more profitable". This is not always the case. You can be having 50% occupancy, but charging premium prices – which means that you will attract better quality guests, have less turnover of people (cleaner will clean less, amortisation of the property will be less) and your overall headache will be less. Whereas if you are having high levels of occupancy (90% - 100%), you might be underselling your property at a very cheap rate, getting some "dodgy" people on the way and having more cleanings to be done (your cleaner will be happy as she will be making more cash), but you have a higher chances of getting more problems – remember the saying "more people = more problems!".

So if you are averaging a 75% monthly stays and you have that 3 – 4 single nights in between – will that extra £500 (on an average) be something you can live without or are you willing to take the risk on it? The choice is yours!

We personally allow 1x night stays to all of our previous gusts that we had not had a problem with hosting for longer stays and also for family and friends that we know are not going to damage the property. Also depending on what our monthly revenue target is, we might allow a 1x night stay in some of the properties that are not that central, that are more in the outskirts of the city where not a lot is happening and you know that the likelihood of a guest throwing a party isn't that high. It all depends on your tolerance levels and your risk against reward ratio.

Tip #39 – VAT And When To Charge It?

In the UK there is a threshold of £85,000 for business that offer a service (such as trading), which the Furnished Holiday Lets a.k.a. Short Term Rentals/Serviced Accommodation. If you exceed that amount in terms of annual revenue – you need to start adding the 20% VAT to your nightly rates.

You need to understand that when you are finishing your tax year, you can claim back those 20% as a deductible expense for your business, so it is not that scary, the only thing is that it might affect your nightly rate prices. When you know that your travel agency will take 20% and the taxman will collect another 20% + you still need to pay your expenses for running that unit every single month - you basically are not left with much profit.

There is an organisation called TOMS (Tour Operators Margin Scheme) – which is basically another way to pay your VAT based on the margin you are making within that business. It is a bit complicated to explain here; hence I will tell you more about it in the 2nd Part of this book series. But to understand it simply, you will not have to pay for VAT (so no more 20% per transaction), but pay TOMS (which if your profit margin is 10%, that is how much you will be paying).

When you are starting with your Short Term Rental business the only thing you need to worry about is getting to the £85,000 turnover. Not paying taxes, but just reaching to that annual turnover – when you do, that means that you will be making some good cash. And when you have money in the bank, you can solve more problems. So focus on increasing that monthly revenue, increase that casfhlow and in time, swap your VAT with TOMS to pay even less in tax to the taxman (if you are the taxman reading this book, ignored what I just said and go to the next chapter!).

Tip #40 – Charge A Cleaning Fee or Not?

There was a debate before, saying that if you charge less for your nightly stay, but add that extra amount to your cleaning fee, the travel agency will only tax you on that nightly rate, but not your cleaning fee. So in layman's terms – you will be getting more out of your reservation. But have you actually considered what the guests see first when they click on your property on Airbnb or Booking.com?

A £40 night's stay? That looks good, let me add 2x nights in total for 2x people, let me see how much that will be ... WHAT!?

£170.... for WHAT??

2x nights x £40 = £80

£10x per extra guest per night = £20

cleaning fee = £50

linen fee = £20

Total = £170

So their initial observation that was £40 per night with an intention of paying £80 in total now turned out to be more than twice...

No wonder they would not reserve with you.

One of the options that not many people are doing nowadays is experimenting with including all the cleaning and linen fee and taxes etc into the reservation fee.

So instead of having to see £40 per night, they will see £85 per night. But at least when they go at the check-out page they are not surprised of any "hidden fees". It is something that we have been experimenting with and has proven good success. What you need to do is adapt to the market, see the customers' behaviour, observe how long it takes for them to make a reservation with you and know that the easier and simplified the process the less numbers and add on fees they see, the higher the likelihood of them booking with you and leaving a good review.

Tip #41 – Data Collection – Core of Any Business

Most businesses in today's day and age have a core foundation that their future is built upon – customer database. A business that has 10,000 potential customers is much more desirable than one that has 100. The reason for this is because you can create different marketing campaigns and sales funnels that you can covert a percentage of those 10,000 each month and guarantee consistent business (only from your current database).

The way you collect that database in your Short Term Rental business is quite simple – first you need to establish what type of data/information you require from your guests and what is the reason behind that. Most simple form of information that you need to get from each one is their name, email address, phone number and possibly address. Once you have this you then add that to your CRM system (Customer Relations Manager). Some examples of CRMs are SalesForce, Hubspot, Keap etc.

Then what you or your team can do is divide the gusts in 2x groups – business travellers and leisure travellers. Now when you create marketing campaigns you can have separate emails sent to the different groups, so it targets them more specifically to their needs.

You can even filter it further – based on some of the responses you get from your previous guests (say they will not travel until then next year) – you can postpone/delay those emails and don't send them that often. For others however, you can send aggressive marketing every week (say to people that came to work in your area and have a higher chance of staying with you again).

There is plenty of ways to play around with this, but make sure you collect that information from your guest when they reserve with you! It will add a lot of value to your business and also you will possibly have a less stressful winter season when you know you have the chance to get some direct bookings from your existing database.

Tip #42 – Disappear For a Day

You want to know if what you are doing works? Disappear for a day! Turn off your phone and forget that your business exists.

Have you ever tried this? No? It is a scary thing to even think, isn't it?

Well, If you want to build something that is sustainable, long lasting and not directly dependant on you being actively there – you need to put yourself in those uncomfortable situations, where you know you can check your phone and answer the guest's phone calls and help them give them directions to check-in or you can leave your team deal with this.

I have this belief – weather you are away for 8hrs, full time working, on holiday, sick or whatever, you are not physically present in that business. So, the more often you put yourself in those types of situations, you will understand your business much more and will get a clear picture of what is missing and how can you fix it – do you need more people in the business or more systems? Do you need to have video instructions for check-in or call your cleaner an hour before the guest checks-out to remind them that they have a cleaning to do today? It will be different for any business. But unless you realise that the reason for you being in this industry and taking on short term rentals (most of the time) isn't because you love it (if you do, that helps), but it is because you want to have your time back, to spend with family, friends, get extra income and live a more free life with more choices.

I understand that you need to be physically and mentally present when starting out, but once you start building, you need to give your business some space to breathe, let it go through some difficult moments and see if you have put enough systems in place to get your business to overcome them and prosper.

Many successful CEOs just take a month off vacation and when they come back the business is either still running the same way or doing even better. That is when you know you have made it as a business person.

So whatever you decide to do, understand that as much as you like what you do, you need to let go of some things you have been doing and let your team handle that. You will thank me later!

Tip #43 – Have An Inventory Log In Each Property

What is an Inventory Log you ask? Do you want to systemise your business – is my answer.

What we have started going when we expanded your business beyond 5x properties is have an Inventory Log in each one of them. This consists of the name of the property (or its address) and then list all of the things that are the daily consumables that you are responsible of replenishing after you run out. Those could be – toilet paper, kitchen roll, bin bags, washing up liquid, shower gel, shampoo, conditioner, sponges etc. Anything that you can think of that either the guests or the cleaners use for the property to running sufficiently, we put on the Inventory Log. Right across each item we put down the quantity of it. And to finish off, at the bottom of it we put the date which the cleaning was done and the inventory check was completed.

So after our cleaner finishes cleaning, she checks what we have in our storage area (within each one of our property), writes it down on that Inventory Log, puts the date, takes a photo and sends it to our WhatsApp group chat. This way we keep a track of how we are doing with the quantity, and now when should we re-stock, also keeps us updated of when the property was cleaned and gives us a track record of that properties performance in terms of how much of which item do guests use the most within a period of 30x days. Then we establish how much on an average that property cost us for re-stocking the inventory every month and based on that we can play around with our daily pricing to either increase or decrease, adding that additional cost of the supplies we provide to each guest.

If you have never used this and want to know what is going with your units and keep track of the monthly expenses per each one – an Inventory Log is a great tool to use and implement.

If you want a copy of the template I use, reach out to me via Instagram on nick__kirov and I'll send you one for free!

Tip #44 – Offer FREE Stays!

FREE Stays?? Are you out of your mind?? Who will be paying for my expenses?

Well if you think like that you are right – nobody will, except your clients. But if you want to grow in this industry you need to understand the concept of Giving in order to Receive!

I am not saying that you need to be "gifting" your properties to random people so they can drink, do drugs and destroy your property after that long night of gangbanging... Excuse my French.

Have you ever thought about reaching out to people (most specifically – influencer) on social media, offering them FREE Stay for them to come over, document their stay, post your property on their feed and get those thousands of people see it. Then they put a link to your website – SHABANG! You might just got yourself a random booking just by offering that FREE Stay with that influencer + if you build up a good relationship – they can possibly act as your Travel Agency – they promote your property and by their followers clicking on that link and reserving your property – you offer those influencer a commission out of every booking. It is a WIN-WIN-WIN for all of you!

It is not even that difficult to do – you just target a niche – reach out to those people, be direct and give them an offer they could not refuse (no violence or guns allowed here), if 1 out of 100 accept – boom, you just have a potential Funnel from that one person that has reach and access to thousands if not hundreds of thousands of people watching him.

Also, sometimes you can offer giveaways – doing Facebook offers such as – LIKE, COMMENT, SHARE this post and your name will be added to a hat. After a few days the name I pick up from that hat will receive a 2x night FREE stay with us at our XYZ Apartment! You can get free advertising this way. The opportunities are endless, just step outside that box that you are limiting your mind to, explore what can be done and do it – sacrifice a few nights of your "precious" property for a much greater returns in the future!

Tip #45 – Utilise Social Media

I believe I've touched a bit on this from Tip #44, but let's expand a bit further. Limiting yourself to advertising only on Airbnb and Booking.com tells me that you would like to run this as a hobby rather than grow it like a business.

If you are interested in expanding in this industry and making a name for yourself and your customer to trust and not think twice – you need to establish presence outside of the regular platforms everyone uses. Utilise the tools that are available to almost everyone out there – Facebook, Instagram, LinkedIn, Snapchat, YouTube, OnlyFans etc. Understand that the more that people see your property, they see yourself, the more they are inclined to making a reservation within your website and securing your future profits and allowing you to go out there and get more and more properties!

You can also run paid advertising (which if you are not sure what you are doing, better not throw cash in the air for that – get someone that is experienced in running ads, paid them, pay for the ads and get more actual visitors to your website that are prospects who have a higher chances of reserving your place).

Some platforms you have to be more professional than others – LinkedIn and OnlyFans – you need to present what you are selling in a more elite and desirable concept – talking about LinkedIn here okay!?

On Facebook for example you can be joining different groups for people that travel, relocate in your area, buy and sell groups – start posting there. You might get banned here and there, but consider this – if you make best-friends with the Admins of those groups – you just secured them a commission from each and every booking you get from you posting your website in their group and getting reservations from there. Who would not want that deal, eh?

So to summarise – social media is a massive tool that you need to understand how to utilise for your Serviced Accommodation business. Understand how each platform works, start producing some content, reach out to a few people and make it a WIN-WIN-WIN situation amongst everyone. That is what you need to focus on, rather than only relying on the mainstream travel agencies that everyone uses!

Tip #46 – Give A Property Back

Have you ever thought – what if I have a property that is underperforming or just does not work for you? What if you just break even every month, you have so many maintenance issues you need to resolve and everything that you seem to touch breaks (maybe get your maintenance person to fix it?) and it is causing you a lot of headaches? Finally you have decided to give it back but you are not sure how to go about it?

Well, I will be honest with you – we have never had to return a property as of yet, as most of our properties are in locations that are in high demand and the quality of the building/apartments is 7/10 when we got them – so it is less likely for things to break or underperform. However, if we were to establish that we have a property that we need to give back to the Landlord or Lettings Agent, the first thing I would do is communicate with them and be honest. Remember the break clause we were talking about in Tip #1? If you have secured a 36x month tenancy, you have got a potential break on month 6x (depending how you have structured your contracts). This means that with you giving your Landlord/Lettings Agent the heads up of you wanting to exit out of the contract as soon as month 6x has been reached – they know they can start advertising that property for rent once again. You might be left with 2x more problems then – your furniture (that you have possibly bought) and the future reservations that the guests have got with you.

What will be the best way to fix this problem – it is simple – get yourself another property. Yes, you don't have to sell all the furniture and cancel all future reservations – you can, but that does not mean that you should. As we spoke earlier – are you doing this for a hobby or are you're trying to run a business and secure a legacy for yourself and your family?

With finding another property – make sure that the location is better, condition of the property is better and you have a bit more peace of mind that this one will work. This is exactly why you should never stop looking for the next deal. Because, you never know when you might have to return a property and you would need another one to transfer all bookings and furniture across.

So to keep this short – if you ever feel the need to return a property that does not work for you – never be afraid to do so, just make sure you have a plan B for all of the future bookings and furniture that is in there. Worst case scenario, you sell this as a Packaged Deal to someone new in this game, as a lot of "Deal Sourcers" do, you promise them the Moon and the Stars and the Millions of Pounds that will fall from the sky when they buy this deal from you – and you are out in the clear. And you transferred your problem to someone else. Do not do that, be smart!

Tip #47 – Track Everything

Do you remember that I've told you that you need to be a Control Freak? Now let me delve a bit more in depth about this!

Have you ever been fat (I will cut straight to the point here, no need to be offended when reading this – I am an ex-personal trainer, so I kind of know what I am talking about)? You have realised you got that spare tyre around your waist and you've decided you will go to the gym 3x days a week and you will get in phenomenal shape in no time. You do that. Workout every 3x days for the next few weeks, then you step on the scale, not much has changed. Now you decide you will do 5x workout sessions a week – more is better, right? You do that for another few weeks, and guess what? You BURNOUT.

You have not changed any of your other daily habits – your stress levels, your sleeping pattern, your calorie intake and you expect to see results just by going to the gym?

No my friend – that does not work like that. Being in good shape requires much more than just working out. It is a combination of the things mentioned above – and how do you know if you are making progress? Well, simple – you track everything!

You need to track your daily calorie intake, your sleeping pattern, the levels of stress you get on a daily basis on top of doing your regular 5x day training sessions – to which I am a strong believer that everyone must exercise every single day instead of having 3x days or 5x day working schedules. You might think that you need to get some time for the muscles to recover bla bla – find me on the socials, send me a text and let's have a discussion there.

Getting back to it – when you track all of the above, every single day, every single week and you make small tweaks across time, you will see how you get in shape and the feeling you will get from you getting to an optimal physical shape will be phenomenal. And knowing that you have done all of this by yourself! Awesome.

Now imagine if you can transfer that same mind set about tracking everything and apply it to your business? You will be un-f*cking-stoppable! By tracking how many days your property is booked across a month, which platform do guests stay, what type of guest are you having most (leisure people or business people), how many people stay with you, how many require a car parking, how far in advance do you receive bookings, how much the average nightly reservation, how much is your average nightly price and all of the other metrics that you can track in your business will give you the cutting edge of why you are doing much much better than your competition.

And if I have to be honest, there would not be much competition left, because of how focused and competent you become within your business, you would not mind that other people may be running the same business as you are – they will not be a factor for your success.

Tip #48 – Evicting Guests

Coming down to the fun part – evicting guests? Now I believe it is much easier and better to evict guests than tenants. I have personally done both and would not want to deal with either, however getting guests out is a bit easier (in my experience) than tenants.

Now let us start at the beginning - why would you ever want to evict/kick out guests from your property – well, there a numerous reasons, but let me give you a few. You can find out that the guests are doing illegal business within your property – prostitutes, selling drugs, etc. Nasty sh*t. You might also have guests that throw a party to which you are not invited. Disappointing. You might also have guests that reserve for 1x, but 10x show up. So whatever the situation you are in, you first need to establish was there any red flags during the reservation process that you could have tracked down to avoid any of this happening? May be in your communication with the guest, they were acting aggressively, or avoiding your questions by confirming how many people will be staying or refusing to provide IDs of the people staying etc.

So once you establish what you could have done wrong, discuss with your team, and put a system in place to track for those specific behaviours/patterns for you to avoid getting guests like this.

Second, speak with your guests – call them. If they do not pick up, message them. If they do not reply back, go to the property, or send someone from your team to the property. If they are disrespectful or do not listen to you or your team when you tell them that the other 9x people need to leave, there are no parties allowed inside the apartment, or you would like a free service with a happy ending from them escorts - if all of them refuse, then you get the police involved. What they will do is come to the apartment, you can tell them what is happening, show them that the guests have reserved from XYZ travel agency, provide them with the IDs and tell them that they broke your house rules and they refuse to leave.

Most of the time police officers have dealt with similar situations and will assist you with this. Also, most of the times, your guests would not want you to call the police so they will behave until the rest of the stay or take the party elsewhere. Both way, you will have your property under control and it will be your choice whether or not to keep the guests there or kick them out. Keep in mind that you can still charge them their damage deposit, so that is an extra incentive for you and a bad choice from them if they want to continue with their poor behaviour.

Don't be afraid to kick out the guests that misbehave, but before you do that, ensure that you limit those types of guests entering your properties with putting the right checks and measures in place beforehand.

Tip #49 – Continuous Education

Have you ever wondered even for a second, why are you reading this book and what gives me the right to write it the first place? Well, answer is simple – Continuous Education.

The reason I am where I am now in business is because I never stopped learning and acquiring more knowledge about this business, property investing etc. Exhausting the resources such as reading and listening to books, watching YouTube videos of people that are doing what I wanted to do myself, paying for online courses, attending free and paid networking events, mixing up with people all across the UK and learning from their experiences, their mistakes, their future plans for their businesses and putting me in a position to get a mentor myself and learn from the top dogs in the game – this is why I am writing this lil booklet – giving you a small snippet of what has worked for me in my business, the mistakes I would have avoided only if I knew what to lookout for at the beginning and the things that I am currently testing and doing to grow and expand.

So what I am advising you is this – never stop educating, it does not matter if you are just starting out or you have a few years of experience. There is always something new that you can learn and implement, always someone that you have not spoken to yet, that can change your perspective on this 180°. Surround yourself with people that are likeminded, people that grow together, created partnerships and businesses together and understand that within this industry you cannot succeed alone!

Tip #50 – Workout Every Single Day!

Now without a doubt this was going to be my very 1st tip to you, but I thought that if I started with this, I might confuse you in thinking that you never bought a Short Term Rental Book to learn about fitness and working out?

This tip however, even last in this book – should be first in your life! Working out every single day. Without bragging too much again, but as an ex-personal trainer, understanding how the body works and what effects do physical exercises have on the body and the mood change and endorphin boosts and dopamine hits that you get. It is the superpower that everyone CAN and SHOULD experience every single day.

As the saying goes "Strong body, strong mind!". And that is without a doubt the most important aspect we need to apply to each and every single one of our lives. A workout – does not matter how long it takes – can be a 10x minute session to a 3x hour fully blasted workout – as long as you keep your body active, your blood flowing, your mind sharp – everything else in your life will align – your work, your family, your business. Everything that is important to you – you will have more energy to put into and you will be going within a positive state of mind – that right there can be the barrier that needed removing for you to excel in business and life!

Tell me when was the last time when you've seen someone just finish a good workout session and be negative and angry and annoyed at the world? When? Probably only that guy that believes he is a 'natty', but only he believes in that.

As part of my personal advice to anyone I get in contact with that are interested in going into business or actually being in business – I tell them to workout every single day. And trust me – you will know a motherf*cker that works out every single day – you can clearly tell that just by speaking with them and seeing how they handle themselves. I firmly believe in the saying "How you do anything is how you do everything!".

So, do me a favour – if you haven't worked out today – go and do it, if you are reading this and it is already late – do 100 push ups – if you can't, do 99. Whatever you do, get your body active – your mind will be thanking you big time!

Conclusion

Alright, time to sum this book up. All in all, I hope you managed to get a lil bit of value out of what you just read. When I read books I mainly search for that 1x golden nugget out between the pages. That 1x golden piece of advice that I can take with me and implement in my life or business that will make a difference with at least 1%. You don't need to be making massive changes every single day. You just need that 1% improvement every single day – that improvement in your business, in your career, in your relationship in your health, in your business.

Challenge yourself. Challenge yourself to be 1% better every day. Do it for 1x year. And to make things a bit more interesting – document your journey. Document that 1% that you are getting better every single day. And then on the last 365th day I want you to watch the video you shot on day 1. Tell me – do you recognise that person? Would you be happy if 365 days later you were still that same person?

As one of my mentor says – "Success is a by-product of Personal Development" and "Your levels of success will never exceed your levels of Personal Development". So, if you think you deserve to have more money in your bank account or be respected amongst your peers or have a good loving partner. Ain't none of that true – if you don't become the person you are most proud of, you will never attract any of the things you desire.

I have started my journey in 2018. I have documented every single step – the good times and the bad times. I know we are in the conclusion section of this book, but f*ck it. Got one last piece of advice I want to share with you and I believe I have already hit a bit of it earlier. It is to document your journey. I want you to grab your phone, flip the camera around and start talking – what date is it today, where are you in life, what are the things you are struggling with, what have been your successes so far, what are your future plans... EVERYTHING. I want you to document everything – and take this – you don't need to upload those videos anywhere. Keep them for yourself. On your phone. You don't have to share them with anyone. These videos that you make – whenever you are sad, frustrated, pissed off, happy, excited etc – these videos you will be watching continuously throughout your journey. And after a year or two – you will look back and see how you've come. How many people you have met along the way, how many people you've helped, how many deals you've done, how much you have changed as a person.

You know what the best bit is? After you make it – and some of you will – you can get to show these videos of your early beginning to your loved ones, to your friends, to the people that doubted – you will get to show them how difficult your journey has been and why you have gone through all of the sh*t to get to the place you are at now – prospering!

The innate feeling of gratitude that you will going through those past videos – will act as a dose of energy that will spike your whole body into seeing for yourself through what you have been through and give your inspiration how the next few years will look if you are going in the same direction you are headed.

And remember – videos, not photos. Those videos will what you can leave for your children – those videos will be the hope that you will gift them – that everything anyone puts their mind, effort, focus and energy into – they can achieve!

Peace out!

Nick Kirov

For more daily inspiration, tips, advice, lessons and more follow me on my socials below:

Facebook: Nick Kirov

Instagram: nick__kirov

Website: www.nick-kirov.com

Vol. 2 To Be Continued...

Printed in Great Britain
by Amazon

27942214R00076